My Year with the Saints

FOR KIDS

Compiled by
Peter Celano

PARACLETE PRESS
BREWSTER, MASSACHUSETTS

2019 First Printing

My Year with the Saints: For Kids

ISBN 978-1-64060-167-3

Library of Congress Cataloging-in-Publication Data
Names: Celano, Peter, compiler.
Title: My year with the saints : for kids / Peter Celano.
Description: Brewster, MA : Paraclete Press, Inc., 2019.
Identifiers: LCCN 2018024140 | ISBN 9781640601673 (trade paper)
Subjects: LCSH: Christian saints—Prayers and devotions—Juvenile literature.
  | Devotional calendars--Catholic Church—Juvenile literature.
Classification: LCC BX2166 .M9 2018 | DDC 242/.62--dc23
LC record available at https://lccn.loc.gov/2018024140

10 9 8 7 6 5 4 3 2 1

Published by Paraclete Press
Brewster, Massachusetts
www.paracletepress.com

Printed in the United States of America

This Book Belongs to

_____

Contents

A Message from Pope Francis
vi

A Message from Pope Francis

Hope to become a saint!

May the Lord grant us all the hope of being saints. But you might ask me: "Father, can someone be a saint in everyday life?" Yes, you can. "But does this mean that we have to pray all day?" No, it means that you have to do your duty all day. . . . But you have to do everything with a heart open to God, so that at work, even in sickness and suffering, even amid struggles, your heart is open to God. This is how we can become saints.

May the Lord give us the hope of being saints. Let us not think that it is something difficult, that it is easier to be scoundrels than saints! No. We can become saints because the Lord helps us; He is the one who helps us.

[Becoming a saint] is the greatest gift that each one of us can give to the world. May the Lord grant us the grace to believe so deeply in Him that we become the image of Christ for the world.

—POPE FRANCIS,
from an address given at his weekly general audience,
June 21, 2017

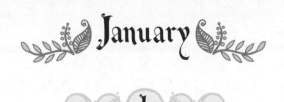

January

1

We begin today with the greatest of the saints, the Blessed Mother, the Virgin Mary. Today, the Solemnity of Mary, the Mother of God, is an occasion to pray one of the oldest prayers we have. There is no better way to begin a new year than by asking Mary to pray for us.

Hail Mary, full of grace, the Lord is with thee; blessed art thou among women, and blessed is the fruit of thy womb, Jesus.
Holy Mary, Mother of God, pray for us sinners,
now and at the hour of our death. Amen.

2

St. Basil the Great loved poor people with very special intentions. He also loved prayer, manual work, and living in community.

"When someone steals another's clothes, we call them a thief. Should we not give the same name to one who could clothe the naked and does not?"
—St. Basil the Great

Pray for me, St. Basil.

Only fear the Lord and serve him faithfully with all your heart.
For consider what great things he has done for you.
—1 SAMUEL 12:24 (ESV)

Dear God, I want to serve you.
What will be my service for you today?

Holy Scripture tells us that who we are, what we do, and what we see, is important. "Don't you know that you . . . are God's temple and that God's Spirit dwells in your midst?"
—1 CORINTHIANS 3:16 (NIV)

God, I realize what a responsibility I have to live for you!
Please help me today.

"You cannot be half a saint; you must be a whole saint
or no saint at all."
—ST. THÉRÈSE OF LISIEUX

Oh God, I want to be a saint. I do! But how? Please show me how!

Remember this, when you go to Mass, you are meeting Jesus Christ. Meditate upon this truth:

> "When you approach the tabernacle remember that he has been waiting for you for twenty centuries."
> —St. Josemaría Escrivá

How does meeting Christ regularly help you to become a saint?

> "From silly devotions and sour-faced saints, good Lord, deliver us!"
> —St. Teresa of Avila

Don't try to look so serious when you are doing God's will. Smile! Laugh, sometimes. The saints teach us that God wants our obedience *and* our joy.

Be kind to one another, compassionate, forgiving one another as God has forgiven you in Christ.
> —Ephesians 4:32 (NAB)

*Dear God, thank you for friends. And please help me, today—
to be a better friend.*

9

"Love God, serve God; everything is in that."
—ST. CLARE OF ASSISI

What do saints mean when they say that "everything" is in loving God and serving others? They are repeating something important that Jesus taught—do you know where in the Gospels Jesus said that?

How will you love and serve God, today?

10

This is probably the most important principle of prayer to learn:

"Whether we receive what we ask for, or do not, we should still continue steadfast in our prayers—because to fail in obtaining the desires of our heart, if it's God's will that we not obtain them, is for our good. For we don't know what God knows, and we don't know what is really profitable for us."
—ST. JOHN CHRYSOSTOM

11

St. Francis of Assisi taught his spiritual brothers and sisters— in other words, people who want to become saints—to develop their passion and desire for God in the Eucharist.

"What the poor man does at the rich man's door, or the sick person in the presence of his physician, or someone who is thirsty at a flowing stream, I do before the Eucharist. I pray. I adore. I love."
—ST. FRANCIS OF ASSISI

"Holy Communion is the shortest and safest way to heaven."
—POPE ST. PIUS X

Lord, I know about going to Mass, but now I'm asking, please prepare me to know you in a whole new way when I take Holy Communion.

Each of the sacraments are important for our salvation. Do you know about "sacraments"?

The Sacrament of Reconciliation (Confession) helps to repair our relationship with God, and prepares us for heaven. Self-honesty is the beginning.

"We will either accuse ourselves or excuse ourselves."
—ST. JOHN VIANNEY

January

"If a man wishes to be sure of the road he treads on, he must close his eyes and walk in the dark."

—St. John of the Cross

God, I sometimes have no idea where I'm going. But I know that you are here with me, and even when it feels like I'm walking in the dark, I know that you're in the lead, in front of me.

Look for those portions of the Bible that talk about love. Saints have said that the whole message of the Bible is God's love for us. This is why our whole lives are meant to be love.

"Love is the most necessary of all virtues. . . . It is much the same with the word of God. If it is spoken by someone who is filled with love and charity—the fire of love of God and neighbor—it will work wonders."

—St. Anthony Mary Claret

Rest in this knowledge today, from St. Padre Pio:

"Our Lord loves you and loves you most tenderly. If he is not letting you feel the sweetness of that love, it is because he wants to make you more humble."

—St. Pio of Pietrelcino

Today is the feast day of St. Anthony the Great. He is sometimes called the Father of All Monks. He encourages us to keep working at becoming saints. We can do it!

"I pray that we should use every effort to press on toward this life's goal. Let no one look behind him as did Lot's wife. . . . To look back means to have second thoughts. . . . Do not fear the word 'virtue' as if it were unattainable."

—St. Anthony

"I am amazed when people say they are speaking with God by reciting the Our Father even while they are thinking of worldly things. When you speak with a Lord so great, you should think of who it is you are addressing and what you yourself are, if only that you may speak to him with proper respect."

—St. Teresa of Avila

Give God the Father your full attention today in prayer.

If I give everything I own to the poor and even go to the stake to be burned as a martyr, but I don't love, I've gotten nowhere. So, no matter what I say, what I believe, and what I do, I'm bankrupt without love.

—1 Corinthians 13:3 (msg)

I want to do more for you, God. Make me on fire with your love today, O Lord.

20

"[Love] is a choice, a preference. If we love God with our whole hearts, how much heart have we left? If we love with our whole mind and soul and strength, how much mind and soul and strength have we left? We must live this life now."
—DOROTHY DAY

Who am I supposed to love today, Lord?
Please show me—and make it as obvious as possible!

21

"Above all, I was growing in the love of God. In my heart I felt upward impulses that I had not known until then. Sometimes I was truly transported by love."
—ST. THÉRÈSE OF LISIEUX

Dear God, I want to grow in Your love so much!

22

The saints often say that the beginning of prayer is gratitude.

O give thanks to the LORD, for he is good;
for his steadfast love endures forever.
—PSALM 107:1 (NRSV)

Pray: *I am thankful today, Lord, for. . . .*

"In all created things discern the providence and wisdom of God, and in all things give God thanks."

—St. Teresa of Avila

Make a list today. (Even if you make the list in your head.) Look around you; what do you see that makes you thankful?

"No Christian duty is more urgent upon us than to give thanks."

—St. Ambrose of Milan

Most of us who pray the Lord's Prayer regularly are not searching for our daily bread each day. We usually have plenty to eat. Compose your own version of the Prayer today, praying for each of the things we ask for, but making each one into a statement of thanks and gratitude.

St. Gregory Nazianzen died on this day in Cappadocia, which is today part of the country of Turkey. He was a fourth century archbishop of Constantinople.

"Give something, however small, to the one in need. For it is not small to one who has nothing. Neither is it small to God, if we have given what we could."

—St. Gregory Nazianzen

We spend our whole lives learning to pray.

"Prayer is an aspiration of the heart, a glance in the direction of heaven, a cry of gratitude, and love and joy in the middle of trials."

—St. Thérèse of Lisieux

If you live with intention for God each day, you will surely be made fun of from time to time. It's true! Don't let it bother you too much. St. Paul said, "we are fools for the sake of Christ" (1 Cor. 4:10 nrsv). St. Ignatius of Loyola said, "Out of gratitude and love for him, we should desire to be reckoned fools."

You're in holy company if you're ever made fun of for doing God's work!

Today is the feast day of a man known as perhaps the greatest theologian in the history of the Catholic Church. He was brilliant, and many of his writings became a part of our Catechism. Nevertheless, this same smart man is the one who said:

"All the efforts of the human mind cannot exhaust
the essence of a single fly."
—St. Thomas Aquinas

If I speak in the tongues of mortals and of angels, but do not have love, I am a noisy gong or a clanging cymbal.

—1 Corinthians 13:1 (nrsv)

Dear God, show me how to love with your love, today.

You are special to God. Know that truth wherever you are, today.

"As the sun shines simultaneously on tall cedars, as well as on each little flower, as if each flower was the only one on earth, in the same way our Lord is concerned particularly for every soul as if there is no other one like it."

—St. Thérèse of Lisieux

Pope Saint John Paul II was our Holy Father from 1978 to 2005. He was a beloved Pope, and one of the most important people of the twentieth century. Maybe you've learned about him in school. He had a great ministry to the kids of the Church. John Paul II taught all Catholics to:

"Remember the past with gratitude. Live the present with enthusiasm. Look forward to the future with confidence."

—Pope St. John Paul II

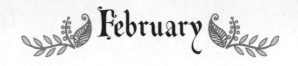

February

"You learn to speak by speaking, to study by studying, to run by running, to work by working, and just so, you learn to love by loving. All those who think to learn in any other way deceive themselves."

—St. Francis de Sales

Give me the courage, Lord, to put my faith into practice this day.

Do you ever hear your parents worrying out loud? Do your teachers talk about worries that are preoccupying them? Adults worry; it is true. We all worry way too much.

"Pray, hope, and don't worry," said St. Pio of Pietrelcino. Give your worries to God.

Pray: *Dear God. . . .*

"Pure love . . . knows that only one thing is needed to please God: to do even the smallest things out of great love—love, and always love."

—St. Maria Faustina Kowalska

Who will you show love to, today?

Remember to love the people around you throughout the day today—as one saint said, "first of all, in your own house."

"Spread love everywhere you go: first of all, in your own house. Give love to your children, to your wife or husband, to a next-door neighbor. . . . Let no one ever come to you without leaving better and happier. Be the living expression of God's kindness; kindness in your face, kindness in your eyes, kindness in your smile, kindness in your warm greeting."

—St. Teresa of Calcutta

"The proof of love is in the works. Where love exists, it works great things. But when it ceases to act, it ceases to exist."

—Pope St. Gregory the Great

If you say you love God but you don't love others, you may not love God after all.

What are you most "attached to" these days? What things or people or activities most preoccupy your time?

> "The things that we love tell us what we are."
> —St. Thomas Aquinas

Dear God, I want to spend more time with you.
I want to show you that I love you.

"What does love look like? It has the hands to help others. It has the feet to hasten to the poor and needy. It has eyes to see misery and want. It has the ears to hear the sighs and sorrows of men. That is what love looks like."
—St. Augustine of Hippo

I will show my love for others with hands, feet, eyes, and ears today.

Open your Bible and read 1 Corinthians chapter 13 today.

Then, reflect on what St. Thérèse of Lisieux once wrote in a letter: "My director, Jesus, does not teach me to count my acts, but to do everything for love, to refuse him nothing, to be pleased when he gives me a chance to prove to him that I love him."

9

"Lord, grant that I might not so much seek to be loved
as to love."
—ATTRIBUTED TO ST. FRANCIS OF ASSISI

To know God is to love others. This is more important than
feeling love ourselves.

10

If you don't feel loved by God today (we don't always *feel* it),
take that as a sign that God wants you to learn something more
important.

"Our Lord loves you and loves you tenderly, and if he does not let
you feel the sweetness of his love, it is to make you more humble
and abject in your own eyes."
—ST. PIO OF PIETRELCINO

11

"We must love our neighbor as being made in the image of God
and as an object of his love."
—ST. VINCENT DE PAUL

When you see that kid at school who bothers you, try and see
him/her as someone loved by God.

February

If there is someone you don't love, or that you don't even like, you need to pray more. Pray. Now.

> "Love, to be real, must cost—it must hurt—
> it must empty us of self."
> —ST. TERESA OF CALCUTTA

"What a weakness it is to love Jesus Christ only when he caresses us, and to be cold immediately once he afflicts us. This is not true love. Those who love thus, love themselves too much to love God with all their heart."
> —ST. MARGARET MARY ALACOQUE

Lord, I will love you every day. Please show me how.

Yes, there really was a St. Valentine (*Valentinus*, in Latin), but we know nothing about him for certain. For various reasons, the early Church linked his life and reputation with love. But given the historical uncertainty, the Church removed him from the general calendar of saints in 1969.

What Christ said about love is absolutely certain: "You shall love the Lord your God with all your heart, with all your soul, with all your mind, and with all your strength. . . . You shall love your neighbor as yourself. There is no other commandment greater than these"

—MARK 12:30–31 (NAB)

"Do everything quietly and in a calm spirit. Do not lose your inner peace for anything whatsoever, even if your whole world seems upset."

—ST. FRANCIS DE SALES

Do you have something difficult you have to do, today? Offer that difficulty up to God in prayer.

Today is the feast day of St. Juliana, virgin and martyr. Juliana lived in the time of the Roman Empire when a young girl would be betrothed (promised in marriage) to an older man, even if it was against her will. Well, Juliana became a follower of Christ, and was baptized secretly because her father was pagan. He didn't approve. When her wedding approached, she refused. Her father was angry and handed her over to the local governor, who was also her former fiancé, to be killed.

St. Juliana, pray for me,
that I may be courageous in my faith as you were.

February

Are you experiencing something difficult today? If you are, know this:

"The same everlasting Father who cares for you today will care for you tomorrow and every day. Either he will shield you from suffering or give you unfailing strength to bear it."
—St. Francis de Sales

Fish live best in plenty of water. People live best when they live with lots of prayer.

I am like a fish today, God,
wanting to spend time in your cool, dark waters.

"Love is patient, love is kind."
—1 Corinthians 13:4 (NAB)

Dear God, teach me your love today. I am trying!

20

"Almost the soul's whole work is to realize its unworthiness to receive such great good and to occupy itself in thanksgiving."
—St. Teresa of Avila

All prayer might be summarized as giving thanks. If you are praying mostly for yourself—asking God for things you don't have—then start praying today with thanks instead. Thank God for what you have, for who you are, for your family, your school, your. . . .

21

God's there, listening for all who pray,
for all who pray and mean it.
—Psalm 145:18 (msg)

How often do you pray and not really mean it? How often do you pray only because other people tell you to pray? It is time to begin praying because you want to.

22

"Do you think that because we cannot hear God, he is silent? He speaks clearly to the heart when we beg him from our hearts to do so. . . . He is always right at our side."
—St. Teresa of Avila

Dear God, Our Father. . . .

February

Try not to be someone who complains that it's Monday, or that it's raining, or that some other small thing is bothering you. Listen to a saint:

"The truly patient person doesn't complain of his hard lot or desire to be pitied by others. He speaks of his sufferings in a natural, true, and sincere way, without complaining or exaggeration."

—St. Francis de Sales

"Little children follow and obey their father. They love their mother. They know nothing of covetousness, ill-will, bad temper, arrogance and lying. This state of mind opens the road to heaven. To imitate our Lord's own humility, we must return to the simplicity of God's little ones."

—St. Hilary of Poitiers

Kids usually want so desperately to grow up, and fast! But the Bible says, the faith of a child is the truest kind of faith. What do you think that means? (Read Matthew 18:1–5, as you consider this.)

Do you have trouble at home? Sometimes it is necessary to talk with a counselor at school, an older friend, or your priest. At all times, know this:

"The many troubles in your household will tend to your edification, if you strive to bear them all in gentleness, patience, and kindness. Keep this ever before you, and remember constantly that God's loving eyes are upon you."
—St. Francis de Sales

"Open your minds and hearts to the beauty of all that God has made and to His special, personal love for each one of you."
—St. Pope John Paul II

Take a minute today to write down the ways that God has shown his love for you. Share with someone what you've written.

"I got this," people often say, to show that they are in control of what's about to happen. Of course, it's never true. We are not in control. But with God, we truly have "got this."

"Do not become upset when difficulty comes your way. Laugh in its face and know that you are in the hands of God."
—St. Francis de Sales

During this season of Lent, we could learn a lot from the saints. If you are finding Lenten fasting and other small sacrifices to be difficult, listen to this saint:

"I have no taste for corruptible food nor for the pleasures of this life. I desire the bread of God, which is the flesh of Jesus Christ, who was of the seed of David; and for drink I desire his blood, which is love incorruptible."

—St. Ignatius of Antioch

"You must ask God to give you power to fight against the sin of pride which is your greatest enemy—the root of all that is evil, and the failure of all that is good. For God resists the proud."

—St. Vincent de Paul

What pride are you holding onto? Do you really believe that God can't see it?

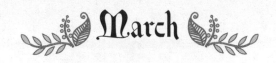

March

"If you don't know what you're doing, pray to the Father. He loves to help. You'll get his help, and won't be condescended to when you ask for it. Ask boldly, believingly, without a second thought. People who 'worry their prayers' are like wind-whipped waves. Don't think you're going to get anything from the Master that way, adrift at sea, keeping all your options open."
—JAMES 1:5–8 (MSG)

What more is there to say? Pray, now. And be honest with God!

Pope Francis praised the American monk and spiritual writer Thomas Merton in 2013 when he spoke before a joint session of the U.S. Congress.

Pray today with Thomas Merton:
"For now, oh my God, it is to You alone that I can talk, because nobody else will understand. . . . I hear You saying to me . . . 'I will give you what you desire. . . . I will lead you by the way that you cannot possibly understand.'"

"Be glad when you are blamed.
In time, you will see what gains your soul experiences."
—St. Teresa of Avila

This is a hard lesson to learn and accept.

*Dear God, thanks for reminding me
that small sufferings can teach me a lot.*

"Even if the whole world blames you, what does it matter as long as you are in God's arms? He is powerful enough to free you from everything; only once did he command the world to be made and it was done."

—St. Teresa of Avila

As I go about my day today, God, I will remain "in your arms."

"God is love, and those who abide in love abide in God,
and God abides in them."
—1 John 4:16 (nrsv)

Show love today to someone who wouldn't expect it from you. Surprise them!

6

"During the time ordained for prayer, the devil is apt to arrive in the soul, causing much more conflict and trouble than when the soul is not occupied in prayer. He does this so that holy prayer may become tedious to the soul. He tempts the soul often with these words: 'This prayer avails you nothing.'"
—St. Catherine of Siena

There are dangers in the world, even, or especially, from what we cannot see. Don't allow the devil to trip you up!

7

On this day in 1274, St. Thomas Aquinas died in a monastery in Italy, where he was trying to recuperate from an illness. Since his death, he has been acknowledged as one of the smartest people ever to write books of theology. Still, he once said: "Love takes up where knowledge leaves off," which means, you can't ultimately "know" your way to God.

You have to love God first and foremost.

We read six special Psalms during Lent each year. They are called the Six Penitential Psalms. The first of them is Psalm 6. Pause to pray these words more than once throughout the day, today.

> The Lord has heard my supplication;
>> the Lord accepts my prayer.
> All my enemies shall be ashamed and struck with terror;
>> they shall turn back, and in a moment be put to shame.
>> —PSALM 6:9–10 (NRSV)

The next Penitential Psalm is number 32. Pray these powerful words today, and remember to go to Confession.

> Then I acknowledged my sin to you,
>> and I did not hide my iniquity;
> I said, "I will confess my transgressions to the LORD,"
>> and you forgave the guilt of my sin.
> Therefore let all who are faithful
>> offer prayer to you;
> at a time of distress, the rush of mighty waters
>> shall not reach them.
>> —PSALM 32:5–6 (NRSV)

This is a season to uncover our sins. We shouldn't try to hide them. We of course can never hide our sins from God. Pray today with the writer of the third Penitential Psalm:

> I confess my iniquity;
> I am sorry for my sin.
> —PSALM 38:18 (NRSV)

From the last of the Penitential Psalms:

> Teach me to do your will,
>   for you are my God.
> Let your good spirit lead me
>   on a level path.
> For your name's sake, O LORD, preserve my life.
>   In your righteousness bring me out of trouble.
>   —PSALM 143:10–11 (NRSV)

What will you do, today, to show God that you are turning away from your sin?

On this day in 1622, Pope Gregory XV canonized Teresa of Avila, the great Spanish mystic and theologian, author of books such as *The Interior Castle*.

"Oh, my Lord! When I think of the many ways you suffered, I do not know what to say for myself. I don't know what I must have been thinking when I wished for no suffering or what I am doing when I make excuses for myself. For what is it to you, Lord, to give much rather than little? I do not deserve it, but I have not deserved the favors you have already shown me. How can it be that I should want others to think well of someone so evil as me, when they have said such wicked things about you, who are good above all other good? It is intolerable, my God."
　　　　　　　—St. Teresa of Avila

"The whole world is not worth one soul."
　　　　　　　—St. Francis de Sales

Who will you help, today? Who will you feed, or clothe, or comfort? With whom will you share the Good News of God's love?

Are you facing temptation? Satan is real, and wants to stop you from your love of God.

Listen to a saint: "The soul tries hard to cling to God by an act of will. With God's permission, Satan goes even further: hope and love are put to the test. These temptations are terrible."

—St. Maria Faustina Kowalska

Eight days ago we read that St. Thomas Aquinas, after writing lots of books of theology, said, "Love takes up where knowledge leaves off." You're in school; can you think of any subject you study in school for which love is more important than knowledge? There isn't one. Knowing God is different than knowing anything else in life.

Love is its own kind of knowledge, when it comes to God, and love of God leads to serving him in ways that simply studying about God, does not. Loving God and serving Christ teaches us more about faith than reading books—even books like this one you are reading this very minute—ever could.

Today is the feast day of St. Abraham Kidunaia. He was born in Edessa, part of what is today the country of Turkey. Abraham decided to devote his entire life to serving God in prayer and good works. His parents were rich, and when they died, they left him lots of money. He gave it all away to the poor.

St. Abraham, pray for me.

You've probably heard of St. Patrick's Day. Just about everyone has! But few people know anything about St. Patrick. Few people know, for instance, that he wasn't Irish. He was English. He also wasn't the first missionary to Ireland, but he was the most important.

> Christ be with me, Christ within me,
> Christ behind me, Christ before me,
> Christ beside me, Christ to win me,
> Christ to comfort me and restore me,
> Christ beneath me, Christ above me,
> Christ in quiet, Christ in danger,
> Christ in hearts of all that love me,
> Christ in mouth of friend and stranger.
> —ST. PATRICK

On this feast day of St. Cyril of Jerusalem, one of the great theologians of the early Church, remember what Cyril said: "Since Christ Himself has said, 'This is my body,' who shall dare to doubt that it is his body?"

Are you attentive when you go to Mass? Are you showing reverence for the Eucharist?

Angels are all around.

"Make yourself familiar with the angels and behold them frequently in spirit; for without being seen, they are present with you."

—St. Francis de Sales

What angels are near you, today?

"The way Jesus shows you is not easy. Rather, it is like a path winding up a mountain. Do not lose heart! The steeper the road, the faster it rises towards ever wider horizons."

—Pope St. John Paul II

I won't complain when the way is tough, Lord.
I know that if it weren't tough, it wouldn't be worthwhile.

Today is the feast day of St. Nicholas of Flüe, a hermit and ascetic from the fifteenth century who is also the patron saint of Switzerland. Nicholas was a man of prayer who also counseled world leaders. It is said that a war was once avoided because of his wise, spiritual advice given to leaders of both sides in the conflict.

St. Nicholas, show me how to be a peacemaker.

"The future is in your hearts and in your hands. God is entrusting to you the task, at once difficult and uplifting, of working with Him in the building of the civilization of love."
—POPE ST. JOHN PAUL II

What will you do, today, to help "build the civilization of love"?

"Jesus is with you even when you don't feel His presence. He is never so close to you as He is during your spiritual battles. He is always there, close to you, encouraging you to fight your battle courageously. He is there to ward off the enemy's blows so that you may not be hurt."
—ST. PIO OF PIETRELCINA

Whatever you are struggling with, Jesus is there for you. Call on him.

Don't look for comfort when you serve God. It doesn't always work that way.

"True . . . devotion consists in serving God without experiencing any sensible consolation. This means serving and loving God for His own sake."
—ST. PIO OF PIETRELCINA

Today is the Feast of the Annunciation to the Blessed Virgin Mary.

St. Augustine says: "Mary was happy [because] she heard God's word and kept it." She believed the angel who said that she would bear a son, becoming the Mother of God—Jesus.

I will say "yes" to you today, God.

Sometimes kids find it easier to understand the Blessed Virgin Mary's faith than adults do. "She heard God's word and kept it," as St. Augustine said yesterday. That is so true!

Go to a Bible and read the account of what's called The Visitation, in Luke 1:39–56.

St. Louis de Montfort had a great passion and devotion to Mary.

"Pray with great confidence, with confidence based upon the goodness and infinite generosity of God and upon the promises of Jesus Christ. God is a spring of living water which flows unceasingly into the hearts of those who pray."
                          —St. Louis de Montfort

28

On this day in 1515, St. Teresa of Avila was born in Avila, Spain. Knowing much about the life and Passion of Jesus, she said, "We always find that those who walked closest to Christ were those who had to bear the greatest trials."

—ST. TERESA OF AVILA

Pray for me, St. Teresa.

29

Are you feeling spiritually "dry" right now? If you are, this may be why:

"[Jesus] wants you entirely for Himself. He wants you to place all your trust and all your affection in Him alone and it is precisely for this reason that He send you this spiritual aridity, to unite you more closely to Him."

—ST. PIO OF PIETRELCINA

Today is the feast day of one of our most interesting saints: John Climacus, who is also admired in the Eastern Orthodox Church. St. John is sometimes called "St. John of the Ladder" because he wrote a book, *The Ladder of Divine Ascent*, detailing how to discipline one's soul and body in order to ascend—or rise up toward—God.

St. John Climacus, pray for me today
as I try to raise my mind and heart to God in all I do.

"Take care, take care never to close your heart to anyone."
—St. Peter Faber

Peter Faber is the Jesuit saint you've never heard about. Ignatius of Loyola and Francis Xavier—they are the Jesuits saints most people know. But Peter Faber was special. Together with Saints. Ignatius and Francis, Faber founded the Society of Jesus (Jesuits) in the early sixteenth century in France. Ignatius was a bold former soldier, a leader who commanded attention. Xavier was a daring missionary, traveling across oceans to evangelize people in China and India. In contrast, Peter Faber was quiet; he listened well; he refused to give up on people; he was a man of prayer. If you ever meet a Jesuit, ask him his favorite Jesuit saint and he might just say St. Peter Faber.

St. Peter Faber, pray for me today.

April

Today is the feast of St. Theodora, who died at the hands of the Romans in about the year 120, when it was against the law to be a Christian. She helped her brother, St. Hermes, while he was in prison, and before he was murdered and martyred for his faith. Then, she, too, was martyred. It isn't as difficult to be a Christian today, as it once was!

I will be a witness for you today, Lord.

Today is the feast day of St. Mary of Egypt. If you think you've made mistakes, or that you are a great sinner, pray to St. Mary, because she was a notorious sinner before she found Christ. It was while contemplating an icon of the Blessed Virgin that she was convicted of her sin. Then she left for the desert to do penance and live virtuously.

St. Mary of Egypt, pray for me.

Mother Theodora once said, "A devout man happened to be insulted by someone, and he said to the person, 'I could say as much to you, but God's commandment keeps my mouth shut.'"
—*The Wisdom of the Desert Fathers and Mothers*

Dear God, I need your help. . . .

Today is the feast of St. Isidore of Seville, who is considered one of the "Fathers of the Church."

"Prayer purifies us, reading instructs us. Both are good when both are possible. Otherwise, prayer is better than reading."
—ST. ISIDORE OF SEVILLE

"We are not born Christians, we become Christians."
—TERTULLIAN

What do you think this quote from Tertullian, who was one of the early Church Fathers, means? Were you born into a Christian family? Are you "becoming" a Christian?

April

6

"God deliver us from saying, 'We are not angels,' or 'We are not saints,' whenever we commit some sin. We may not be. But, what a good thing it is for us to reflect that we can be if we will only try and if God gives us his hand. Do not be afraid that he will fail to do his part if we do not fail to do ours."

—St. Teresa of Avila

Don't "give in" to your sin easily. Expect great things of yourself. You can stop doing that thing you shouldn't do, and it can become a new habit *not to do it*!

7

Is this your prayer for today?

"O my Lord, inflame my heart with love for You, that my spirit may not grow weary amidst the storms, the sufferings and the trials. You see how weak I am. Love can do all."

—St. Maria Faustina Kowalska

Pray the St. Maria prayer in your own words, now.

Be a witness for Christ today wherever you go. But remember that you can't argue a friend into faith.

St. Thomas Aquinas, one of the Church's greatest theologians, once said: "To one who has faith, no explanation is necessary. To one without faith, no explanation is possible."

St. Agnes of Rome died as a martyr at the young age of thirteen. At a time when Christianity was illegal, she was killed by the Roman government for being a follower of Christ.

"Christ made my soul beautiful with the jewels of grace and virtue. I belong to Him whom the angels serve."
—St. Agnes of Rome

"We must always have courage, which God gives to the strong. He will give courage to you and to me."
—St. Teresa of Avila

Dear God, without excuses, I'll live for you today.

April

One of our collects (that's another word for prayers) in church after Easter begins with this:

"May your people exult for ever, O God, in renewed youthfulness of spirit, so that, rejoicing now in the restored glory of our adoption, we may look forward in confident hope to the rejoicing of the day of resurrection."

How are you "exulting" today?

"Dear young people, let yourselves be taken over by the light of Christ, and spread that light wherever you are."
—POPE ST. JOHN PAUL II

Kids are often the ones who best of all "spread" God's light in the world. How will you do that wherever you are going today?

Don't get stuck today on your sin. Remember God the Father's great love for us. Listen to the words of a saint:

"We are not the sum of our weaknesses and failures; we are the sum of the Father's love for us and our real capacity to become the image of his Son."
—POPE ST. JOHN PAUL II

Today is the feast day of a little-known saint, Blessed Peter González, OP, a Spanish friar and priest who lived at the same time as Saints Francis of Assisi and Dominic Guzman, famous saints and founders of the Franciscan and Dominican orders. Peter decided to devote his life to Christ one day after he was riding his beautiful, fancy horse and it bucked and dumped him, in all his fine clothes, into a mud puddle.

Blessed Peter, pray for me today, that it won't take embarrassment for me to realize how worthless I am without God.

"Have patience with all things, but chiefly have patience with yourself. Do not lose courage in considering your own imperfections but instantly set about remedying them—every day begin the task anew. Our entire good consists not only in accepting the truth of God's word, but in persevering in it."
—St. Francis de Sales

Dear God, I will persevere (meaning, I'll keep trying, when it's difficult) today in. . . .

This is important for kids to learn and remember! Listen to St. John Bosco:

"Fly from bad companions as from the bite of a poisonous snake. If you keep good companions, I can assure you that you will one day rejoice with the blessed in Heaven; whereas if you keep with those who are bad, you will become bad yourself, and you will be in danger of losing your soul."

—St. John Bosco

Before I formed you in the womb I knew you, before you were born I set you apart.

—Jeremiah 1:5a (NIV)

Every single person is unique, beautiful, and loved by God. Remember that today, for yourself. And remember this also, today, if you see someone who is being mistreated by others. You can make sure that someone else, too, knows that God loves them.

"Every day you give yourself to us, representing yourself in the sacrament of the altar, in the body of your holy Church. What has done this? Your mercy. Oh, divine mercy! My heart

suffocates in thinking of you, for everywhere I turn my thoughts, I find nothing but mercy."
—St. Catherine of Siena

Rest for a moment in God the Father's love. Take a few minutes to write down how that feels.

Hear my voice, Lord, when I call;
have mercy on me and answer me.
—Psalm 27:7 (NAB)

Have you ever had a painful experience that prompted you to change something about your life? What was it, and how did it change you?

"For the soul to come to unite itself perfectly with God through love and will, it must first be free from all desire of the will, however slight. It must not intentionally and knowingly consent with the will to imperfections, and it must have power and freedom to be able not so to consent intentionally. The soul will eventually reach the stage of not even having these desires, for they develop out of a habit of imperfection."
—St. John of the Cross

Give me strength today to do what I should do,
and to not do what I know I shouldn't do.

April

The Gospel tells us this about Mary, after the archangel told her she would become the Mother of God. "[Jesus Christ's] mother treasured all these things in her heart" Luke 2:51 (NRSV). What are you treasuring in your heart?

Pray for me, Holy Mother of God.

Here is a famous prayer from St. Richard of Chichester: "May I know thee more clearly, love thee more dearly, and follow thee more nearly, day by day."

Lord, this is my prayer today. I want to know you more clearly; I want to love you more dearly (than any person, any thing, in the world), and I want to follow you more nearly, this day, and always.

This is the feast day of St. George, who is most often represented in art slaying a dragon. He was a Roman soldier and a Christian martyr, known for tremendous courage.

St. George, pray for me, that I may be courageous in the face of evil, just as you were.

On this day in 1581, St. Vincent de Paul was born in southwestern France. Have you ever been to a St. Vincent de Paul Shop or soup kitchen? He dedicated his life to serving the poor.

> "Charity is certainly greater than any rule. Moreover, all rules must lead to charity."
> —St. Vincent de Paul

Kids are often the best at caring for the poor. Kids understand better than adults what it feels like to be left out or excluded. Consider this: that *excluded* is often how a poor person feels.

> "Charity is that with which no man is lost, and without which no man is saved."
> —St. Robert Bellarmine

> "Apart from the cross, there is no other ladder by which we may get to heaven."
> —St. Rose of Lima

Nothing you have or own can ever help you when it comes to heaven. God is not impressed by anything but faithfulness.

I will be faithful to you today, God, by. . . .

On this day in 2014, Pope John Paul II was canonized by Pope Francis. John Paul II was probably Pope when your parents were kids. Ask them about him. Pope John Paul II was one of the most influential people in the world—not just in the Catholic Church—during his lifetime.

> "Darkness can only be scattered by light,
> hatred can only be conquered by love."
> — POPE ST. JOHN PAUL II

The Franciscan saints are some of our most eloquent examples of choosing poverty—in all that "poverty" means—in following Christ. St. Francis of Assisi, the first Franciscan, insisted on giving away everything he had in order to follow Christ.

We don't usually give away everything we have to be Christians, today. But still, consider for a moment: what would it mean for you to practice "poverty" more in your life?

29

St. Anthony of Padua was an early Franciscan saint. He was a friend of St. Francis.

"The creator of the heavens obeys a carpenter, the God of eternal glory listens to a poor virgin. Has anyone ever witnessed anything comparable to this?"

—St. Anthony of Padua

30

One form of "poverty" can be to stop being overly proud of ourselves and our gifts and talents. It is good to thank God for gifts of intelligence, but not good to be haughty about them.

"Let the philosopher not look down his nose at the common person, but listen to him. The wise should listen to the simple. The educated should listen to the illiterate. Children of princes, listen to peasants."

—St. Anthony of Padua

May

God doesn't want us to be afraid of him. God wants us to love him. The Bible says: "There is no fear in love. But perfect love drives out fear, because fear has to do with punishment. The one who fears is not made perfect in love."
—1 JOHN 4:18 (NIV)

I will serve you today in love, without fear.

You are the salt of the earth.
—MATTHEW 5:13A (NAB)

Try to be like Mary today. What does that mean? When God revealed to Mary that she would bear a son and he would be the Messiah, she believed. Then she faithfully did what the angel told her to do. She was like "the salt of the earth." Salt is what gives everything flavor, life, taste, goodness! Be like Mary today. How will you "salt" the earth around you?

"Do not be afraid that [God] will fail to do his part if we do not fail to do ours. Do not let there be anything we know of that would serve the Lord and that, with his help, we would not do.

We must always have courage, which God gives to the strong. He will give courage to you and to me."

—St. Teresa of Avila

Where do you need courage, today? What are you facing that frightens you? Pray to God: *I won't make excuses, God. You are beside me.*

"All the great truths of religion, the mysteries of eternity, plunged my soul into a happiness that was not of earth. I was already feeling what God reserves for those who love Him (not with the human eye, but with that of the heart), and seeing that eternal rewards have no proportion to the slight sacrifices of life, I wanted to love, love Jesus with passion, give Him a thousand signs of love while I could still do it."

—St. Thérèse of Lisieux

I want to know you better, Lord.

So here's what I want you to do, God helping you: Take your everyday, ordinary life—your sleeping, eating, going-to-work, and walking-around life—and place it before God as an offering.

—Romans 12:1 (MSG)

Transform me today, Christ. Make me more like you.

God said to St. Catherine of Siena: "The soul should not say its vocal prayers without joining them to mental prayer. That is, while you are reciting vocal prayers, you should endeavor to elevate your mind in my love."

You are in my heart and mind. I'm not only praying, God; I'm listening.

Don't forget to pray today.

"A soul arms itself by prayer for all kinds of combat. In whatever state the soul may be, it ought to pray."
—St. Maria Faustina Kowalska

Jesus Christ, please be my shield today.
Let me know that you are by my side.

The saints were courageous risk-takers.

"If the highest aim of a captain were to preserve his ship, he would keep it in port forever."
—St. Thomas Aquinas

Lord, I want to take a risk for you today. Show me what I should do.

9

"Totally love him who gave himself totally out of love for you."
—ST. CLARE OF ASSISI

Wherever you go today, and whatever you do, remember that God loves you with an extravagant love.

10

Your eyes will see the king in his beauty; they will behold a land that stretches far away.
—ISAIAH 33:17 (NRSV)

"I am not asking you to become involved in long and subtle meditations with your understanding and reason. I am only asking you to look at Christ. Who can prevent you from turning the eyes of your soul upon this Lord?"
—ST. TERESA OF AVILA

11

[Jesus said,] "If I'm telling the truth, why don't you believe me? Anyone on God's side listens to God's words."
—JOHN 8:46–47A (MSG)

I'm listening to you, God. What you say, I believe.

Beloved, we are God's children now; what we will be has not yet been revealed. What we do know is this: when he is revealed, we will be like him, for we will see him as he is.
—1 JOHN 3:2 (NRSV)

"What will it be like when we receive Communion in the everlasting dwelling of the King of heaven?"
—ST. THÉRÈSE OF LISIEUX

"Then he came to the disciples and found them sleeping; and he said to Peter, 'So, could you not stay awake with me one hour?'"
—MATTHEW 26:40 (NRSV)

This verse from the Gospel of Matthew describes what happened in the Garden of Gethsemane, where Jesus went to pray before he was taken away to be crucified. Jesus asked his disciples, who were nearby in the Garden, to stay awake with Jesus while he prayed. They couldn't stay awake—they couldn't pay attention—for that short amount of time.

14

"[Christ] looks upon you [from the Cross] with his lovely and compassionate eyes, full of tears. In comforting your grief he will forget his own because you are bearing him company in order to comfort him and turning your head to look upon him."
—St. Teresa of Avila

I am here, Lord. I'm awake. I'm watching. I'm listening.

15

"It is Jesus who stirs in you the desire to do something great with your lives, the will to follow an ideal, the refusal to allow yourselves to be ground down by mediocrity, the courage to commit yourselves humbly and patiently to improving yourselves and society, making the world more human and more fraternal."
—Pope St. John Paul II

What do you want to do with your life? What will you do with your life—for God?

"It is Jesus that you seek when you dream of happiness; He is waiting for you when nothing else you find satisfies you; He is the beauty to which you are so attracted; it is He who provoked you with that thirst for fullness that will not let you settle for compromise."

—POPE ST. JOHN PAUL II

What you love to do, can also be what you do for God. What makes you happy, can also be what makes God happy.

Pope Pius XI canonized Thérèse of Lisieux on this day in 1925, less than 28 years after she died in France at the young age of 24.

"God . . . wants to call to Himself the littlest and weakest of all. He . . . is pleased to show His goodness and His power by using the least worthy instruments. But Jesus knew how weak I was, and it was for that reason that He hid me first in the cleft in the rock."

—ST. THÉRÈSE OF LISIEUX

Don't love the world's ways. Don't love the world's goods. Love of the world squeezes out love for the Father. Practically everything that goes on in the world—wanting your own way, wanting everything for yourself, wanting to appear important—has nothing to do with the Father. It just isolates you from him.

The world and all its wanting, wanting, wanting is on the way out—but whoever does what God wants is set for eternity.
—1 JOHN 2:15–17 (MSG)

Look around you and consider: what is different between "the world" and what God wants? How can you help?

St. Vincent Ferrer was a Dominican friar who lived in 1300s. He was both a missionary and a philosopher (a really smart guy!).

"Do you desire to study to your advantage? Let devotion accompany all your studies, and study less to make yourself learned than to become a saint. Consult God more than your books, and ask him, with humility, to make you understand what you read. Study fatigues and drains the mind and heart. Go from time to time to refresh them at the feet of Jesus Christ under his cross."

—ST. VINCENT FERRER

"If you truly want to help the soul of your neighbor, you should approach God first with all your heart. Ask him simply to fill you with charity, the greatest of all virtues; with it you can accomplish what you desire."

—ST. VINCENT FERRER

Show me, Lord, how to help my friends today.

21

"I shall love You, I shall love You always; when day breaks, when evening turns into night, at every hour, at every moment; I shall love You always, always, always."
—St. Gemma Galgani

If you want to be a saint, you need to keep finding ways to love others. How can you love someone today?

22

Saints aren't lazy. "You can't be holy if you're not busy," said St. Zita, an Italian woman who lived in the 1200s.

What are you doing for God today? Are you keeping busy with God's work?

23

How do you express yourself creatively? Do you write stories, draw pictures, play an instrument, or build things? Our creativity is a way of honoring God, who inspires us.

"A human being is a vessel that God has built for himself and filled with his inspiration so that his works are perfected in it."
—St. Hildegard of Bingen

24

"If you are suffering trials, or are sad, look upon him on his way to the Garden. What terrible distress he must have carried in his soul, to describe his own suffering as he did and not to complain about it. Or look upon him on the cross, full of pain, his flesh torn to pieces by his great love for you. How much he suffered: persecuted by some, spit upon by others, denied by his friends with no one to defend him, frozen with the cold, left completely alone."

—St. Teresa of Avila

I won't leave you alone, Lord. I'm here.
Even if I don't know what to say, I'm here with you.

25

[Jesus said,] "Whoever wants to be great must become a servant. Whoever wants to be first among you must be your slave. That is what the Son of Man has done: He came to serve, not to be served.

—Mark 10:44–45 (msg)

God, teach me kindness, graciousness, and humility today.

May the eyes of [your] hearts be enlightened, that you may know what is the hope that belongs to [the Father of glory's] call, what are the riches of glory in his inheritance.

—EPHESIANS 1:18 (NAB)

The "riches of glory" are Heaven. They are also the Kingdom of God—and it is our job as Christians to do what we can to bring about God's Kingdom. We do that by loving others and repairing the world.

"Those into whose souls the Lord has already infused true wisdom do not value this love, which lasts only on earth, for more than it is worth. Those who take pleasure in worldly things, delights, honors, and riches will judge it of some value if their friend is rich and can afford to bring them worldly pleasures. Those who already hate all this will care little or nothing for such things. If they have any love for such a person, it will be a passion that he may love God so as to be loved by God. They know that no other kind of affection can last and that this kind will cost them dearly. For this reason they do all they possibly can for the good of their friend. They would lose a thousand lives to bring him a small blessing. Oh precious love . . !"

—ST. TERESA OF AVILA

Give me the courage today, Father, to represent you.

"The brothers praised a monk before Antony. When the monk came to see him, Antony wanted to know how that same monk would bear insults. Seeing that he could not bear them at all, Antony said to him, "You are like a village magnificently decorated on the outside, but destroyed from within by robbers."

—*The Wisdom of the Desert Fathers and Mothers*

Search me, God, and find what is false in me. I trust you.

Jesus answered them, "In this godless world you will continue to experience difficulties. But take heart! I've conquered the world."

—Matthew 16:33 (msg)

Listen to a saint: "Don't let yourselves grow weary. Do not be seduced by pride in your achievement. 'For the sufferings of this present time are not worth comparing with the glory about to be revealed to us' (Rom. 8:18). No one, once he has rejected this world, should think he has left behind anything important. The entire earth, compared to the infinity of the heavens, is small and limited."

—St. Antony, as told by St. Athanasius

30

Do you remember the story of the Israelites wandering in the wilderness for forty years? (See the Book of Numbers in the Old Testament.) At one point, while wandering, the people complained about the food they had to eat. They didn't like it, so God sent them manna from heaven (see Numbers 11:1–9).

What are you complaining about today? Try turning your complaining into gratitude. Even after receiving "the bread of angels" from God (see Psalm 78:25), the Israelites went back to complaining about their food!

31

This is the last day of the "month of Mary." Since ancient times, Christians have celebrated Mary every May, which is also the month of flowers and blossoms in the northern hemisphere. May is when new things grow!

Look around you today and see what's growing, what's blooming, and when you see the beauty of all those flowers, ask Mary to pray for you. (There are lots of flowers and plants named for Mary, too: the Madonna Lily, Lady's Mantle—look them up sometime!)

June

1

"Remember that true humility consists in being ready for what the Lord wants to do with you and happy that he should do it, and in considering yourselves unworthy to be called his servants."
—ST. TERESA OF AVILA

You don't normally think of a "servant" as something you would want to be, do you? But that's what the saints teach us: we should *want* to be the servants of God!

2

"Our labor here is brief, but the reward is eternal. Do not be disturbed by the clamor of the world, which passes like a shadow. Do not let false delights of a deceptive world deceive you."
—ST. CLARE OF ASSISI

God, no matter what happens to me, I will keep my focus on you.

"The Lord ate from a common bowl and asked the disciples to sit on the grass. He washed their feet with a towel wrapped around his waist—he who is Lord of the universe!"
—St. Clement of Alexandria

Practice humility today. Don't show off. Do something for someone else and keep it a secret between you and God.

Spend less time today worrying about how you look, and how you appear to others, and focus only on how you appear to God.

"It is not your outward appearance that you should beautify, but your soul, adorning it with good works."
—St. Clement of Alexandria

"The most beautiful and stirring adventure that can happen to you is the personal meeting with Jesus, who is the only one who gives real meaning to our lives."
—Pope St. John Paul II

Have a "personal meeting" with Jesus today. You can do that, for instance, in prayer, by reading the Bible prayerfully, or by walking outside and just talking with him.

"You perceive it in the depths of your heart: all that is good on earth, all professional success, even the human love that you dream of, can never fully satisfy your deepest and most intimate desires. Only an encounter with Jesus can give full meaning to your lives."

—POPE ST. JOHN PAUL II

Focus again on that personal "encounter" with Jesus. Would-be saints have those encounters whenever they possibly can!

"If we earnestly endeavor to love Jesus, this alone will drive all fear from our hearts and soul will find that instead of walking in the Lord's paths, it is flying."

—ST. PIO OF PIETRELCINA

Are you worrying about something today? Don't. Let it go, and see how your heart and your soul can fly!

June

The feast of Corpus Christi is celebrated by the Church on a Thursday every year, usually in the month of June. Ask your parents or your priest when it is coming this year. *Corpus Christi* is Latin for "Body of Christ." We honor and celebrate the real presence of Christ in the Mass.

"I have no taste for corruptible food nor for the pleasures of this life. I desire the bread of God, which is the flesh of Jesus Christ, who was of the seed of David; and for drink I desire his blood, which is love incorruptible."
—St. Ignatius of Antioch

Today is the feast day of St. Ephrem. He lived in Syria and wrote many hymns, poems, and sermons.

"Virtues are formed by prayer. Prayer suppresses anger. Prayer prevents emotions of pride and jealousy. Prayer draws into the soul the Holy Spirit, and raises a person to Heaven."
—St. Ephrem the Syrian

"To holy people the very name of Jesus is a name to feed upon, a name to transport. His name can raise the dead and transfigure and beautify the living."

—Blessed John Henry Newman

Pray to Jesus today. Repeat your prayer throughout the day, even if you do it silently in your mind or heart and no one but Jesus can hear you.

Because you have made the Lord your refuge . . .
he will command his angels concerning you
to guard you in all your ways.

—Psalm 91:9a, 11 (nrsv)

What are you worrying about? Trust God. Trust that God will protect you.

"A man would do nothing if he waited until he could do it so well that no one could find fault."

—Blessed John Henry Newman

Is there something that you've been hesitant to start, because you don't know if you'll be good at it? Saints teach us that we have to be courageous—and try.

Today is the feast of St. Anthony of Padua, who was a close friend and associate of St. Francis of Assisi.

"Christ acts like a loving mother. To induce us to follow Him, He gives us Himself as an example and promises us a reward in His kingdom."

—ST. ANTHONY OF PADUA

Pray for me, St. Anthony.

St. Junipero Serra was a Franciscan and one of the first missionaries to the Native people of California, before California became part of the United States.

"All my life I have wanted to be a missionary. I have wanted to carry the gospel message to those who have never heard of God and the kingdom he has prepared for them."

—ST. JUNIPERO SERRA

"[Someone who truly loves] will live on earth as if it were heaven, where enjoying a kind of serenity, and weaving for himself innumerable crowns! Such a person will keep his own soul pure from envy, wrath, jealousy, pride, vanity, evil lusts, every profane love, and every bad temper. I tell you, even as no one would consciously injure himself, so too, neither would such a person who loves like this ever desire to injure his neighbors. The loving person shall stand with Gabriel himself even while he walks on earth. This is the profile of one who has love."

—St. John Chrysostom

God, make me a more loving person today.

[St. Peter said,] "Lord, you know that I love you." [And Jesus replied,] "Feed my lambs," [and] "Tend my sheep."

—John 21:15–16 (NAB)

"He who works miracles and has perfect knowledge without love, even though he may raise ten thousand from the dead, will not profit much by it if he is broken off from all others and not endeavoring to mix himself up with any of his fellow servants. For no other cause than this did Christ say that the sign of perfect love toward himself is loving one's neighbors."

—St. John Chrysostom

I need new ways to love friends and strangers, Lord. Show me.

June

"Be careful about your inner thoughts, especially if they have to do with rank. May God, by his Passion, keep us from dwelling such thoughts as: 'But I am her senior'; 'But I am older'; 'But I have worked harder'; 'But that other sister is being treated better than I am.' If you have these thoughts, you must quickly stop them. If you allow yourselves to dwell on them, or introduce them into your conversation, they will spread like the plague and in religious houses they may give rise to great abuses. Pray fervently for God's help in this matter."
                                            —St. Teresa of Avila

Does your mind wander to where you don't want it to go? Do you have trouble paying attention and staying awake in prayer? Ask God to help you.

[Jesus said] "For truly I tell you, if you have faith the size of a mustard seed, you will say to this mountain, 'Move from here to there,' and it will move; and nothing will be impossible for you."
                                            —Matthew 17:20 (nrsv)

Have you ever seen a mustard seed? It is very tiny—but then it grows into a huge plant!

June

Bless the LORD, O you his angels,
you mighty ones who do his bidding,
obedient to his spoken word. . . .
Bless the LORD, O my soul.
—PSALM 103:20A, 22B (NRSV)

You are not spirit only, like an angel. But you can praise God like an angel: constantly! Thank God now for something you are grateful for.

Then Jesus told his disciples, "If any want to become my followers, let them deny themselves and take up their cross and follow me. . . . For the Son of Man is to come with his angels in the glory of his Father, and then he will repay everyone for what has been done."
—MATTHEW 16:24, 27 (NRSV)

God sees what we do, and what we don't do. God knows our hearts. Keep this in mind today.

June

"Guardian angels" are not from fairy tales, but from the Bible itself. After Jesus commended the faith of children, and told his adult disciples to be more like children in faith, he said, "Take care that you do not despise one of these little ones; for, I tell you, in heaven their angels continually see the face of my Father in heaven" (Matthew 18:10-11, NRSV).

Guardian angel, watch over me, today.
Thank you, God, for my guardian angel.

Today is the feast day of St. Thomas More. Have you heard or read about St. Thomas's story? You should. He refused to acknowledge King Henry VIII, rather than the Pope, as the head of the Church of England. He was imprisoned by King Henry, and then beheaded. Before going to his execution, he said, "I die the King's good servant, and God's first."

Consider this question today: Are you serving God first and foremost?

"Tribulation is a gift from God—one that he especially gives His special friends."
—St. Thomas More

Help me in my trials today, Lord, and pray for me, St. Thomas More.

"If honor were profitable, everyone would be honorable."
—St. Thomas More

Examine your motivations, today. Is it virtue that's motivating your actions? What could you do in some situation to be more honorable?

"Every Christian is called to become a strong athlete of Christ, that is, a faithful and courageous witness to his Gospel. But to succeed in this, he must persevere in prayer, be trained in virtue and follow the divine Master in everything."
—St. Pope John Paul II

Can you see similarities between how an athlete has to train, and how a Christian should "train" in prayer and love?

On this feast day of St. Josemaría Escrivá, Spanish priest, initiator of Opus Dei, author of *The Way*, remember what he said: "Don't you long to shout to those youths who are bustling around you: Fools! Leave those worldly things that shackle the heart—and very often degrade it—leave all that and come with us in search of Love!"

St. Josemaría, pray for me! I am bombarded every day by "those worldly things that shackle the heart"!

When you are outside playing today, or playing a game with friends, or against another team, remember the words of this prayer by one of the most important popes in history:

"Lord Jesus Christ, help these athletes to be your friends and witnesses to your love. Help them to put the same effort into personal asceticism that they do into sports; help them to achieve a harmonious and cohesive unity of body and soul."

—ST. POPE JOHN PAUL II

28

When Jesus rose from the dead, angels were there. The Gospel tells us:

"Mary stood weeping outside the tomb. As she wept, she bent over to look into the tomb; and she saw two angels in white, sitting where the body of Jesus had been lying, one at the head and the other at the feet. They said to her, 'Woman, why are you weeping?'"

—JOHN 20:11–13A (NRSV)

If you remembered that angels are always nearby, the next time you are sad or upset, would it change how you feel?

29

On this day in 1461, Pope Pius II canonized St. Catherine of Siena. She recorded hearing these words from Christ: "You cannot repay the love that I require of you. Therefore, I have placed you in the midst of your brothers and sisters, so that you may do to them that which you cannot do to me. That is, I give you the opportunity to love your neighbor of free grace, without expecting any return. What you do to him, I count as done to me."

For you my body yearns; for you my soul thirsts,
in a land parched, lifeless, and without water.
—PSALM 63:2 (NAB)

What would it mean to be "hungry" or "thirsty"—but not for food or water? What would it mean to be "hungry" or "thirsty" for God?

July

1

The next time someone you don't know, or don't like, asks for help, remember this!

"Do not neglect to show hospitality to strangers, for by doing that some have entertained angels without knowing it."
—HEBREWS 13:2 (NRSV)

2

Father Evagrius once said, "Take away temptations, and no one will be saved."
—*The Wisdom of the Desert Fathers and Mothers*

Dear God, I'm thankful today for the temptations that come my way. I know they will make me stronger.

July

3

"The question about the value of life, about the meaning of life, forms part of the singular treasure of youth. Still more so, when youth is tested by personal suffering, or is profoundly aware of the suffering of others; when it comes face to face with the mystery of sin, of human iniquity. Christ's reply is this: 'Only God is good; only God is love.'"

—POPE ST. JOHN PAUL II

Whatever hardships I encounter today,
I know are nothing compared to the suffering of others,
and the love of God.

4

"Yours is the gigantic task of overcoming all evil with good, always trying amidst the problems of life to place your trust in God, knowing that his grace supplies strength to human weakness. You must oppose every form of hatred with the invincible power of Christ's love."

—POPE ST. JOHN PAUL II

How can you, today, "overcome evil with good"?

5

"Athletic competition develops some of the noblest qualities and talents in people. They must learn the secret of their own bodies, their strengths and weaknesses, their struggles and breaking points.

They must develop the capacity to concentrate and the habit of self-discipline through long hours of exercise and fatigue as they learn to take account of their own strength. They must also learn how to preserve energy for the final moment when victory will depend upon a burst of speed or a last push of strength."

—ST. POPE JOHN PAUL II

Do you find it easier to concentrate while playing a sport, or competing in a game, than when you are at Mass or concentrating in prayer?

Pope Francis said this in his Easter message of 2013: "Let us be renewed by God's mercy . . . and let us become agents of this mercy, channels through which God can water the earth, protect all creation, and make justice and peace flourish."

How can you show God's mercy today to the people (and creatures) around you?

Our entire lives are centered around recognizing, honoring, and remembering this truth with the way we live our lives: "For God did not send his Son into the world to condemn the world, but that the world might be saved through him" (John 3:17, NAB).

Thank you, Christ, for saving me.

July

8

"I have seen so many souls, seduced by [a] false light, flying like poor butterflies and burning their wings, then coming back toward the true, the sweet light of love that gave them new wings, more brilliant and light, so that they might fly toward Jesus, that Divine Fire 'who burns without consuming.'"

—St. Thérèse of Lisieux

Holy Spirit, show me your truth.
Bring me closer to God the Father, Son, and Holy Spirit, today.

9

So we do not lose heart. Though our outer self is wasting away, our inner self is being renewed day by day.

—2 Corinthians 4:16 (esv)

"The soul becomes nothing other than an altar on which God is adored in praise and love, and God alone is on it. This is why God commanded that the altar on which the Ark of the Covenant was to be laid should be hollow inside: so that the soul may understand how completely empty God desires it to be in order to be an altar worthy of his majestic presence."

—St. John of the Cross

God, I don't want other things. I want you.

10

Jesus came into the world, not as a king, but as the poor son of a carpenter. Throughout his ministry, he reminded his disciples, "Whoever wishes to be great among you must be your servant"
—MATTHEW 20:26 (NRSV).

Show me today, God, where humility is lacking in my love.

11

[B]e kind to one another, compassionate, forgiving one another as God has forgiven you in Christ.
—EPHESIANS 4:32 (NAB)

"Happy are the souls that are loved by [true friends]. Happy the day on which they came to know them. O my Lord, will you grant me the favor of giving me many who have such love for me? Truly, Lord, I would rather be loved by these than by all the kings of the world."
—ST. TERESA OF AVILA

Thank you for my friends.

[Jesus said,] "For if you forgive others their trespasses, your heavenly Father will also forgive you."
—MATTHEW 6:14 (NRSV)

Are you holding any grudges against anyone? Has someone done something to you that you find difficult to forgive or forget? If there someone today that you need to forgive?

On World Environmental Day, Pope Francis said this: "Once our grandparents were very careful not to throw away any leftover food. Consumerism has led us to become accustomed to the superfluous and the daily waste of food, which we are sometimes no longer able to value correctly, as its value goes far beyond mere economic parameters. Note well, though, that the food we throw away is as if we had stolen it from the table of the poor or the hungry! I invite everyone to reflect on the problem."

Pay attention, today, to what you do with extra food, where you put your trash, and how much you eat. Is there something you can do to help those who have less?

We celebrate today the canonization of the "Lily of the Mohawks." St. Kateri Tekakwitha was a Native American member of the Algonquin-Mohawk tribe. Born in upstate New York (before there were any United States), she died near Montreal, in French Quebec. (In Canada, her feast is celebrated on April 17, instead of July 14.) She converted to the Catholic faith at the age of nineteen, and was famous for her devotion to God and for her ascetic practices—which means denying herself things she might enjoy, in order to focus more on prayer and doing good for others.

Pray for me, St. Kateri.

Today is the feast of St. Bonaventure, one of the great, early Franciscans. He was both a mystic and a theologian. He was also the minister-general (or leader) of the Franciscan Order, soon after the death of St. Francis of Assisi.

Pray with St. Bonaventure:
"Pierce, O most sweet Lord Jesus, my inmost soul with the most joyous and healthful wound of your love, and with true, calm, and most holy apostolic charity, that my soul may ever languish and melt with entire love and longing for you."

On this day in 1228, Pope Gregory IX canonized Francis of Assisi, only twenty-one months after Francis died.

"About everything St. Francis did there was something that was in a good sense childish, and even in a good sense willful. He threw himself into things abruptly, as if they had just occurred to him. . . . He never thought of waiting for introductions or bargains or any of the considerable backing that he already had from rich and responsible people. He simply saw a boat and threw himself into it."

—G. K. Chesterton

"For me prayer is a surge of the heart, it is a simple look towards heaven, it is a cry of recognition and of love, embracing both trial and joy."

—St. Thérèse of Lisieux

Pray with more passion today. Look to heaven when you pray. Pray with happiness and joy. You can even ask God for the gift of tears while you pray. Many saints in history have received that gift.

Thomas of Celano, a friend of St. Francis of Assisi and his first biographer, is called a "Servant of God," which means his cause for canonization is being pursued by the Church. These are the stages of canonization: Servant of God Venerable Blessed Saint. Thomas was one of the great Christians of his era.

Pray this prayer of Thomas of Celano:
"Jesus in my heart, Jesus in my mouth, Jesus in my ears, Jesus in my eyes, Jesus in my hands."

Today is the feast day of a woman named St. Macrina the Younger. (Her grandmother was called Macrina the Elder.) St. Macrina was the sister of two famous, smart theologians in the early centuries of the Church. They, too, were saints: Basil the Great and Gregory of Nyssa. St. Macrina refused to date boys or get married because she wanted to devote herself entirely to serving God. At the end of her life she said:

"God, you have made the end of this life the beginning of our true life."

—St. Macrina the Younger

"Small yet strong in the love of God, like Saint Francis of Assisi, all of us, as Christians, are called to watch over and protect the fragile world in which we live, and all its peoples."

—Pope Francis

How can you "watch over and protect the fragile world in which we live"? Do something special today to care for the natural world.

I am content with weaknesses, insults, hardships, persecutions, and calamities for the sake of Christ; for whenever I am weak, then I am strong.

—2 Corinthians 12:10 (nrsv)

"How good God is! . . . How He apportions out trials according to the strength that He gives us."

—St. Thérèse of Lisieux

Dear God, I am content with my hardships.
I know that they must be mine for a reason.

[Jesus said,] "Watch and pray so that you will not fall into temptation. The spirit is willing, but the body is weak."
—MATTHEW 26:41 (NIV)

Lord, don't let me sleepwalk through this day.
Make me more vigilant in serving you.

Today is the feast day of St. Bridget of Sweden. She was a wife and mother to eight children. When her husband died, she founded a religious order of nuns.

"There is no sinner in the world, however much at enmity with God, who cannot recover God's grace by recourse to Mary, and by asking her assistance."
—ST. BRIDGET OF SWEDEN

After they prayed, the place where they were meeting was shaken. And they were all filled with the Holy Spirit and spoke the word of God boldly.
—Acts 4:31 (NIV)

I am here, God. I'm ready to be bold. What do you want me to do?

Christ explained to St. Catherine of Siena: "In many cases I give one virtue to be the chief of the others. That is to say, to one person I will give principally love, to another principally justice, to another principally humility, or a lively faith, or prudence, or temperance, or patience, or fortitude. I could easily have created people possessed of all that they should need both for body and soul, but I desire that one should have need of the other, and that they should be my ministers to administer the graces and the gifts they have received from me."

Holy Father, show me who needs me, and who I need, today.

Take the next several days, during these times of brief prayer and visits with the saints, to thank God. Sometimes we call this "blessing" God, which also means thanking him.

The Book of Psalms, in the Bible, is full of thanks, blessing, and gratitude. "Singing aloud a song of Thanksgiving and telling all your wondrous deeds."

—PSALM 26:7 (NRSV)

I thank you today, Lord, for. . . .

"And now, our God, we give thanks to you and praise your glorious name."
—1 CHRONICLES 29:13 (NRSV)

It is important, not just to thank God for God's gifts to us, but to thank the people who God has put in our lives. Take time today to thank your mom or dad, your sister or brother, your friend, a teacher, a neighbor, a grandparent.

"I will give thanks to the Lord with all my heart;
I will tell of your wonderful deeds."
—PSALM 9:1 (NRSV)

Pray today with St. Teresa of Avila:
"Almost the soul's whole work is to realize its unworthiness to receive such great good and to occupy itself in thanksgiving."

One of the great Catholic theologians of the Middle Ages, Meister Eckhart, said, "The most important prayer in the world is just two words long: 'Thank you.'"

Pause and thank God today. In fact, make a list of the people, things, pets, and places that you are thankful for.

July

30

"We must protect creation for it is a gift which the Lord has given us, it is God's present to us; we are the guardians of creation. When we exploit creation, we destroy that sign of God's love. To destroy creation is to say to God: 'I don't care.' And this is not good: this is sin."

—POPE FRANCIS

Look all around you outside and see what makes up "Creation." Robins, crows, flies, ladybugs, rabbits, snakes, oak trees, grass, weeds. There have been saints who have written songs and poems to praise these aspects of Creation. St. Francis of Assisi used to even talk and preach to the birds!

31

On this feast day of St. Ignatius Loyola, remember his prayer: "Teach us to give and not count the cost."

This is hard to do. How often have you given something to a friend or relative, only to think right away about what they might give you in return? Try today to do what St. Ignatius says: Give something away without any thought of what you want in return. Give simply to give, and serve God.

August

God said to St. Catherine of Siena: "The soul should not say its vocal prayers without joining them to mental prayer. That is, while you are reciting vocal prayers, you should endeavor to elevate your mind in my love."

When you pray today, don't "walk away" from your prayers when you have finished. Instead, "carry" them with you—if not in your pocket, in your heart.

"If God causes you to suffer much, it is a sign that He has great designs for you, and that He certainly intends to make you a saint."

—St. Ignatius of Loyola

Are you suffering somehow today? Give your suffering to God, and know that God will use it to make you stronger.

August

Today is the feast of one of the most important women in the early church—but most people don't even know her name. She is St. Lydia, and she was converted to Christianity in the early years of St. Paul the Apostle's ministry. "The Lord opened her heart to listen eagerly," writes the author of the Book of Acts, and then she and her household were baptized as followers of Christ (Acts 16:14–15, NRSV). This means that St. Lydia was a leader in the church in the first century.

Lord, open my heart. I want to listen eagerly like St. Lydia did.

Today is the feast day of St. John Vianney. He was a French priest who is known as the patron saint of parish priests.

"You cannot please both God and the world at the same time. They are utterly opposed to each other in their thoughts, their desires, and their actions."
—St. John Vianney

Say something encouraging to your priest this week. Tell him you appreciate him. Or, simply, say a prayer for him.

To the King of the ages, immortal, invisible, the only God, be honor and glory forever and ever. Amen.
—1 Timothy 1:17 (NRSV)

"The truly devout person sets his devotion principally on what is invisible. He needs few images and uses few."

—St. John of the Cross

I don't need to see you, God, to praise you.

A new heart I will give you, and a new spirit I will put within you; and I will remove from your body the heart of stone and give you a heart of flesh.

—Ezekiel 36:26 (NRSV)

A stone heart is unwilling and unable to love and learn. A flesh heart is one that's open to new people, feelings and emotions, and most of all, to loving. What sort of heart do you have?

"Those of you who cannot focus your constantly wandering thoughts on God must at all costs form this habit. I know you are capable of it. I also know that the Lord will help you if you approach him humbly and ask him to be with you. If an entire year passes without your obtaining what you ask for, you should be prepared to continue asking. You should never complain about time so well spent. It is possible to form the habit of walking at this true Master's side."

—St. Teresa of Avila

When in doubt, I will praise you.

August

8

Today is the feast day of St. Mary MacKillop. She died more than 100 years ago in Australia, where she founded a congregation of religious sisters who built schools and institutions to help poor people.

"In the trials, annoyances and anxieties we daily experience, may we ever recognize that loving Fatherly hand that only seeks to draw us closer to himself by giving us opportunities to suffer something for him."

—St. Mary MacKillop

9

Evening, morning and noon I cry out in distress, and he hears my voice.

—Psalm 55:17 (NIV)

Listen to a saint: "There are only two ceremonies that [Jesus Christ] taught us to use in our prayers: We are to pray in the secret place of our chamber, where without noise and without paying attention to anyone we can pray with the most perfect and pure heart. He said: When you pray, enter into your chamber and shut the door and pray. Or else he taught us to go to a solitary and desert place, as he himself did, and at the best and quietest time of night."

—St. John of the Cross

"Faith is to believe what you do not see. The reward of this faith is to see what you believe."

—St. Augustine

We can't see God, can we? We can't see the angels that surround us, either. We were not witnesses to the Crucifixion or Resurrection of Christ. But we believe.

Today is the feast day of St. Clare of Assisi, the first female Franciscan. She gave up the securities of a wealthy family and a future that was all planned out for her, in order to follow Christ in the simple, poor way of St. Francis of Assisi.

"Go forth in peace, for you have followed the good road. Go forth without fear, for he who created you has made you holy, has always protected you, and loves you as a mother. Blessed be you, my God, for having created me."

—St. Clare of Assisi

Today is the feast of St. Jane Frances de Chantal. She is the patron saint of forgotten people, widows, and parents who are separated from their children. St. Jane taught this regarding how to pray:

"There is no problem if our prayer is without words, because the success of prayer depends neither on words nor on study. Prayer's success depends on the simple raising of our minds to God, and the more simple it is, the surer it is."
—ST. JANE FRANCES DE CHANTAL

On World Mission Day, Pope Francis recently said: "The Gospel is Good News filled with contagious joy, for it contains and offers new life: the life of the Risen Christ who, by bestowing his life-giving Spirit, becomes for us the Way, the Truth and the Life."

Notice that the Pope said that a Christian's joy is "contagious." In other words, if one person is joyful, another might "catch" it!
Pray: *May others "catch" my joy, Lord!*

Today is the feast day of St. Maximilian Kolbe, who was one of the Catholic hero-martyrs of the Holocaust during World War II. If you haven't read about him yet in school or church, you should.

"The most deadly poison of our times is indifference. . . . Let us strive . . . to praise God to the greatest extent of our powers."
—St. Maximilian Kolbe

Pray for me, St. Maximilian, that I will be brave in the face of evil.

"God does not lead us all by the same road. . . . We should not be discouraged, then, and give up prayer or stop doing what the others are doing. The Lord might give us great rewards all at once as he has been giving to others over many years."
—St. Teresa of Avila

Give me strength today, God. I won't give up. I will serve you.

"To convert someone, go and take them by the hand and guide them."
—St. Thomas Aquinas

We don't convince others of the truth of our faith by arguing them into submission. We convince them by being their friends and showing them, by our lives, how we are full of love and joy as followers of Christ.

August

"When a gardener pours out attention on a fruit that he wants to mature before its season, it's never to leave it hanging from the tree, but in order to serve it on a brilliantly set table. It was with such an intention that Jesus poured out His graces on [me,] His little flower."

—St. Thérèse of Lisieux

This saint compared herself to a little flower. Pray: *God, water me today, like a flower, and help me to bloom for you.*

"I believe though I do not comprehend, and I hold by faith what I cannot grasp with the mind."

—St. Bernard

Are there things you don't understand about your faith? Sure, there are! None of us understands everything. Questions are okay. Bring your questions to your parents, your teachers, your priest.

"Take pains to refrain from sharp words. Pardon one another so that later on you will not remember the injury. The recollection of an injury is itself wrong. It adds to our anger, nurtures our sins and hates what is good. It is a rusty arrow and poison for the soul. It puts all virtue to flight."

—Saint Francis of Paola

Our words can be like daggers. We hurt each other so easily with what we say. Be careful with your words, today. Use your words for good.

Today is the feast day of St. Bernard of Clairvaux, one of the most influential people (not just Christians) of the late Middle Ages in Europe. He was a counselor to kings and popes, a theologian, a monk, and an abbot.

"In dangers, in doubts, in difficulties, think of Mary, call upon Mary. Let not her name depart from your lips, never suffer it to leave your heart."

—St. Bernard of Clairvaux

Listen again today to St. Bernard of Clairvaux.

"So that you may obtain the assistance of Mary's prayer, do not stop walking in her footsteps. With her for guide, you will never go astray. And while invoking her, you will never lose heart."

—St. Bernard of Clairvaux

Pray for me today, St. Bernard. Pray for me, Mary!

August

Turn to Mary in your prayers, in your mind and heart, today. Ask her to pray to God on your behalf. God loves to listen to you—and to his Mother.

"As long as Mary is in your mind, you are safe from deception. As long as she holds your hand, you cannot fall. Under Mary's protection you have nothing to fear. If Mary walks before you, you will not grow weary. If she shows you favor, you will reach the goal."

—St. Bernard of Clairvaux

Faith, hope, and love abide, these three; and the greatest of these is love.

—1 Corinthians 13:13 (nrsv)

"There are those who seek knowledge for the sake of knowledge; that's Curiosity. There are those who seek knowledge to be known by others; that's Vanity. There are those who seek knowledge in order to serve; that's Love."

—St. Bernard of Clairvaux

"Neither fear nor self-interest can convert the soul. They may change the appearance, perhaps even the conduct, but never the object of supreme desire. . . . Only love can convert the soul, freeing it from unworthy motives."

—St. Bernard of Clairvaux

Examine your motives for following Christ, today. Are you following God out of love (rather than out of fear, rather than out of habit)?

Today is the feast day of St. Louis IX, who was the king of France in the 1200s. He is known to have combined great zeal for serving God together with great devotion to the Church.

"Be kindhearted to the poor, the unfortunate and the afflicted. Give them as much help and consolation as you can. Thank God for all the benefits he has bestowed upon you, that you may be worthy to receive greater."

—St. Louis IX

"It is better not to allow anger, however just and reasonable, to enter at all, than to admit it in ever so slight a degree; once admitted, it will not be easily expelled, for, though at first but a small plant, it will immediately grow into a large tree."
—Saint Augustine

Every person in the world becomes angry. There is nothing wrong with feelings of anger. Problems happen when we allow our feelings to become actions or words that hurt another person.

When you face a temptation to do what you know is wrong, remember the teaching of the saints.

"On each occasion, I say: 'Lord, thy will be done! It's not what this or that one wants, but what You want me to do.' This is my fortress, this is my firm rock, this is my sure support."
—St. John Chrysostom

On this feast day of St. Augustine of Hippo, remember his advice: "Pray as though everything depended on God. Work as though everything depended on you."

God, I need you so much! I need you every moment of every day.
But I also know that I need to show my love for you
by doing your work in the world. I will!

29

Are you often worried about what people say about you? Do your friends sometimes make fun of you for doing what is right? If so, listen to the teaching of the saints. Here is one from St. Teresa of Calcutta:

"Never bother about people's opinions. Be obedient to truth. For with humble obedience, you will never be disturbed."

30

"It is obedience, which, by the light of faith, puts self-will to death. In a boat of obedience, a person will pass happily through the stormy seas of life, in peace of soul and tranquility of heart."
—St. Catherine of Siena

Most people never realize this truth: The secret to happiness is being faithful to God's will, and obedient to him.

August

One of the strangest saints in history was a Syrian man named Simeon Stylites. He lived near Aleppo, in Syria, a place that's been in the news lately because there is a war, there. Near Aleppo, St. Simeon decided to test his penitence with extreme asceticism. Most notably, he had a tall pillar built and then stood on top of it, making that pillar—about the size of a closet—his home. He remained there alone for nearly forty years!

Why did St. Simeon do this? He wanted to overcome his sinfulness. How should you get away from your sin, today?

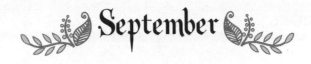

September

BEFORE I FORMED you in the womb I knew you, before you were born I set you apart.

—Jeremiah 1:5a (niv)

Dear God, you know me better than I know myself! I find that both exciting and a bit scary! (I can't hide anything from you!)

[Jesus said,] "Do not judge, so that you may not be judged."
—MATTHEW 7:1 (NRSV)

Dear God, I will not think about what my friends have done wrong. I have enough sins of my own to take care of.

Quick, God, I need your helping hand! The last decent person just went down, all the friends I depended on gone. Everyone talks in lie language; lies slide off their oily lips.
—PSALM 12:1–2 (MSG)

My friends sometimes seem far away, but you, God, are always by my side. Thank you!

September

Today is the feast of St. Rose of Viterbo, a saint of the Church about whom we know very little. She lived in the 1200s and was known for her mystical gifts of prayer and seeing the future.

"Prayer reveals to souls the vanity of earthly goods and pleasures. It fills them with light, strength, and consolation, and gives them a foretaste of the calm bliss of our heavenly home."
—ST. ROSE OF VITERBO

Pray for me, St. Rose.

Today is the feast day of one of the most important and popular saints of the last century. Have you heard of St. Teresa of Calcutta? Before she was canonized by Pope Francis in 2016, she was known as "Mother Teresa." Ask your parents or teachers about her.

"All of us must be saints in this world. Holiness is a duty for you and me. So, let's be saints and so give glory to the Father."
—ST. TERESA OF CALCUTTA

St. Epiphanius used to teach: "Reading the Scriptures is the best way to keep you from sin." Open your Bible today. Take some time reading about God's love for you.

Jesus, I will read my Bible today. I want to grow in my faith.

7

St. Rose of Viterbo died at the age of eighteen. She was strict with herself, denying herself the usual pleasures of childhood, and she gave freely and often to the poor. When she learned that she would die, she said to her parents: "I die with joy, for I desire to be united to God. For those who live well in the world, death is not frightening, but sweet and precious."

Live well in the world today, without fear, united to God.

8

"A saint is not someone who never sins, but one who sins less and less frequently and gets up more and more quickly."
—St. Bernard of Clairvaux

Lord, please make me a saint. I want to be a saint with all my heart, even though I still sin.

9

"Unless we believe and see Jesus in the appearance of bread on the altar, we will not be able to see him in the distressing disguise of the poor."
—St. Teresa of Calcutta

What do you think this teaching of the saints means? Do you see Jesus in the Mass? Do you see Jesus in the face of people who are poor and needy?

September

"I know, God doesn't need anyone to do His work, but just as He allows an able gardener to raise rare and delicate plants, and for that He gives him the knowledge he needs, but reserves for Himself the care to make the plants grow—this is how Jesus wants to be helped in his Divine cultivation of souls."

—St. Thérèse of Lisieux

How will you be God's "hands" in the world today?

Jesus answered and said to her, "If you knew the gift of God and who is saying to you, 'Give me a drink,' you would have asked him and he would have given you living water."

—John 4:10 (NAB)

Pray with St. Catherine of Siena: "Thanks, thanks be to you, supreme and eternal Father, satisfier of holy desires, and lover of our salvation, who, through your love, gave us Love himself."

"The good God does not need years to accomplish his work of love in a soul; one ray from his heart can, in an instant, make his flower bloom for eternity."

—St. Thérèse of Lisieux

I will remember your love for me, Jesus. May that love fill me today, and help me communicate that love to everyone I meet.

Mother Theodora was asked, "If one is habitually listening to bad talk, how can they still live for God alone?" She answered, "Just as when you are sitting at dinner and there are many options of what to eat, you take some but without pleasure. So, when certain conversations come your way, have your heart turned toward God. Listen without really listening."

—from *The Wisdom of the Desert Fathers and Mothers*

Help me tune my heart to you today, Lord.

St. Kateri Tekakwitha was canonized by Pope Benedict XVI in 2012. She is the patron saint of the environment, people in exile, and Native Americans.

Are you concerned for the environment? Do you have a love for creatures—birds, dogs, cats, rabbits? St. Kateri knew these creatures. She was a Mohawk Indian and a Catholic.

Pray for us, St. Kateri. Show us how to better love all God's creatures.

[Jesus Christ] is living, being, spirit, all verdant greening, all creativity. This Word manifests itself in every creature."
—ST. HILDEGARD OF BINGEN

Dear God, you are in all my creativity. Inspire me with your Spirit!

September

"The more I contemplate God, the more God looks on me. The more I pray to him, the more he thinks of me too."
—St. Bernard of Clairvaux

Do you "contemplate" God ever, throughout the day? You don't have to be in church, or at Mass, to do so. Spend some time today thinking about God, praying to God, just quietly whispering or talking with him.

Today is the feast day of St. Hildegard of Bingen. She founded convents, wrote theological books, and was an expert in her era on the subjects of plants and medicines. She was also a mystic and often misunderstood by others. Long considered a saint by some in the Church, since she died in 1179, she wasn't officially declared a saint until 2012, when Pope Benedict XVI officially canonized her. He also declared her a "Doctor of the Church."

Pray for me today, St. Hildegard. I am also sometimes misunderstood.

Remember to read the Gospels. Open your Bible today and read from Matthew, Mark, Luke, or John.

"In the mighty power of God, who is both God and human, and in every place—for his power extends everywhere—the faithful must be empowered by the four Evangelists, pondering God's precepts and filled with virtuous prudence, so that they may understand from where they've come and what they will become."

—St. Hildegard of Bingen

The angel said to me, "Write this: Blessed are those who are invited to the marriage supper of the Lamb." And he said to me, "These are true words of God."

—Revelation 19:9 (NRSV)

"I was growing in the love of God. In my heart I felt upward impulses that I had not known until then. Sometimes I was truly transported by love."

—St. Thérèse of Lisieux

I want to grow in your love, Lord. I want deeper connections to you.

Give thanks to the Lord, for he is good;
for his steadfast love endures forever.

—Psalm 107:1 (NRSV)

"Almost the soul's whole work is to realize its unworthiness to receive such great good and to occupy itself in thanksgiving."

—St. Teresa of Avila

September

"You are all trees of love, and without love you cannot live, for you have been made by me for love. The soul who lives virtuously places the root of its tree in the valley of true humility, but those who live miserably are planted on the mountain of pride."
—St. Catherine of Siena,
recalling words God spoke privately to her

I am reminded today, God, that true happiness comes from being close to you.

Bow down in worship . . . kneel before the Lord who made us.
—Psalm 95:6 (NAB)

Are you comfortable kneeling before God? You should be. By kneeling we show reverence and honor to God. If you do this only at Mass, consider kneeling privately, too, perhaps right now as you pray.

Today is the feast day of St. Padre Pio, also known as St. Pio of Pietrelcina. He was known to be a great counselor to people in spiritual distress. He said many, very wise things.

"We have close to us an angelic spirit who never leaves us for an instant from the cradle to the grave, who guides and protects us like a friend or a brother."
—St. Pio of Pietrelcina

"You must have boundless faith in the divine goodness, for the victory is absolutely certain."
—St. Pio of Pietrelcina

Pray for me, St. Padre Pio—
pray for me to have "boundless faith"!

"You complain because the same trials are constantly returning. But look here, what have you to fear? Are you afraid of the divine craftsman who wants to perfect His masterpiece in this way? Would you like to come from the hands of such a magnificent Artist as a mere sketch and no more?"
—St. Pio of Pietrelcina

Are you suffering in some small way? Or you feeling "down" today? What have you really to fear?

"When we suffer, Jesus is closer to us."
—St. Pio of Pietrelcina

Dear God, I know that whatever I'm suffering from right now
will only bring me closer to you.

September

Today is the feast day of St. Vincent de Paul, a priest who lived 400 years ago and was known for his humility, compassion, and generosity.

"You must ask God to give you power to fight against the sin of pride which is your greatest enemy—the root of all that is evil, and the failure of all that is good. For God resists the proud."
                    —St. Vincent de Paul

Is pride standing in your way and keeping you from serving God?

Remember your experience of kneeling, yesterday.

I saw the Lord sitting on a throne, high and lofty; and the hem of his robe filled the temple. Seraphs were in attendance above him; each had six wings: with two they covered their faces, and with two they covered their feet, and with two they flew. And one called to another and said: "Holy, holy, holy is the Lord of hosts; the whole earth is full of his glory."
                    —Isaiah 6:1–3 (nrsv)

Kneel again, and pray.

People who die and go to heaven are saints. Angels were created by God before human beings. And yet, some angels are

September

also recognized as saints. There are myriad (that word means "countless"—you can't even count them there are so many!) angels, but only a few who are recognized as saints. Today is called Michaelmas, or the feast of St. Michael and All Angels.

I am in your presence right now, God.
The angels are always aware of your presence.
To you are all glory and honor.

On the feast day of St. Jerome, one of the first great scholars and theologians of the Church, remember what he said: "Ignorance of Scripture is ignorance of Christ."

If you are not reading your Bible daily, consider dedicating yourself to that practice, today. Pope Francis recently encouraged all young people to read the Gospels for two minutes each day. Only two minutes! "Read it for two minutes," he said. "You'll see how it changes your life."

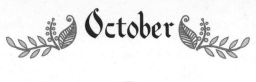

October

Today is the feast day of St. Thérèse of Lisieux.

"Jesus . . . placed before my eyes the book of nature [and] I understood that all the flowers that He created are beautiful. The brilliance of the rose and the whiteness of the lily don't take away the perfume of the lowly violet or the delightful simplicity of the daisy. I understood that if all the little flowers wanted to be roses, nature would lose its springtime adornment, and the fields would no longer be sprinkled with little flowers. So it is in the world of souls, which is Jesus's garden. He wanted to create great saints who could be compared to lilies and roses. But He also created little ones, and these ought to be content to be daisies or violets destined to gladden God's eyes when He glances down at His feet. Perfection consists in doing His will, in being what He wants us to be."

—St. Thérèse of Lisieux

Today is the feast day of Guardian Angels. In the Bible, angels deliver messages. In our lives, they watch over us and protect us.

> Little children, let us love, not in word or speech,
> but in truth and action.
> —1 John 3:18 (nrsv)

Guardian Angels, protect me. God, show me who to love, today.
Remind me to see You in the faces of everyone I see.

In the evening of October 3, 1226, St. Francis of Assisi died.

> Lord, make me an instrument of Your peace;
> Where there is hatred, let me sow love.
> Where there is injury, pardon.
> Where there is doubt, faith.
> Where there is despair, hope.
> Where there is darkness, light.
> Where there is sadness, joy.
> —attributed to St. Francis of Assisi

Today is the Feast Day of St. Francis of Assisi, the most popular saint, other than Mary, in the history of the Church.

"I, Brother Francis, a worthless and sinful man, your little servant, bring you greetings in the name of him who has redeemed and washed us in his precious blood. When you hear his name, adore it with fear and reverence, prostrate on the ground, for he is the Lord Jesus Christ, 'Son of the Most High,' blessed forever!"
—St. Francis of Assisi

October

If I keep my eyes on G<small>OD</small>, I won't trip over my own feet.
—P<small>SALM</small> 25:15 (M<small>SG</small>)

Dear God, help me keep my eyes on You today.

St. Catherine of Siena heard from God: "Another thing is necessary for you to be pure, and to arrive at union with me: You should never judge the will of another person in anything that you may see done or said by anyone, either to you or to others. You should consider my will alone, both in them and in yourself."

Dear God, remind me not to judge.

This is how St. Teresa of Avila taught her nuns to pray the Our Father and the Hail Mary:

"Who could be a better Companion than the Master who taught you the prayer you are about to say? Imagine that this Lord himself is at your side and look at how lovingly and humbly he teaches you. You should stay with such a good Friend for as long as you can before you leave him. If you get used to having him at your side, and if he sees that you love him to be there and are always trying to please him, you will never be able to send him away and he will never fail you. He will help you in all your trials and you will have him everywhere. It is a great thing to have such a Friend beside you."

If I give away all my possessions, and if I hand over my body so that I may boast, but do not have love, I gain nothing.
—1 CORINTHIANS 13:3 (NRSV)

*Dear God, help me not to love my things so much
I want to love you so much more!*

Today is the feast day of Blessed John Henry Newman, an English poet and theologian, who converted from Anglicanism to Roman Catholicism.

"To live is to change, and to be perfect is to have changed often."
—BLESSED JOHN HENRY NEWMAN

October

I concentrate on doing exactly what you say—
I always have and always will.
—Psalm 119:112 (MSG)

Your attention is drawn to many things throughout the average day. Friends. School work. Parents. Activities. Sports. Fun. Chores. How much time do you take each day to remember to pray, or to simply spend time in quiet before God? Do that today. Make it your practice to fit two minutes each day into your schedule to concentrate on him.

"I trust the Lord to help me say a few words that will assist those who have set out on the road of virtue but make no progress as they pass through the dark night to divine union."
—St. John of the Cross

Reveal to me, Lord, what to say to people today.

"Even if the whole world blames you, what does it matter as long as you are in God's arms? . . . His love for those who hold him dear is not weak; he shows us in every possible way. Why, then, do we not show him our highest love?"
—St. Teresa of Avila

God, you love me. I know that, and that's all that matters to me.

October

Do not conform yourselves to this age but be transformed by the renewal of your mind, that you may discern what is the will of God, what is good and pleasing and perfect.
—ROMANS 12:2 (NAB)

Pause, throughout the day today, and ask God to show you the way.

"Your love for me is still imperfect, and your neighborly love is so weak, because the root of self-love has not been properly dug out."
—ST. CATHERINE OF SIENA, listening to God speaking to her soul

May there be less of me and more of You, God.

October

Today is the Feast Day of St. Teresa of Avila

"If you are suffering trials, or are sad, look upon him on his way to the Garden. What terrible distress he must have carried in his soul, to describe his own suffering as he did and not to complain about it. Or look upon him on the cross, full of pain, his flesh torn to pieces by his great love for you. How much he suffered: persecuted by some, spit upon by others, denied by his friends with no one to defend him, frozen with the cold, left completely alone. . . . He looks upon you with his lovely and compassionate eyes, full of tears. In comforting your grief he will forget his own because you are bearing him company in order to comfort him and turning your head to look upon him."

—St. Teresa of Avila

God, investigate my life; get all the facts firsthand. I'm an open book to you; even from a distance, you know what I'm thinking. You know when I leave and when I get back; I'm never out of your sight.

—Psalm 139:1–3 (msg)

You can't hide from God. Why does anyone ever think that they can?! So, be honest with him. What do you need to tell God, today?

Today is the feast of St. Ignatius of Antioch, one of the very first martyr saints of the Church. He was born in about AD 35, just a couple of years after the death and resurrection of Christ. St. Ignatius was a great defender of the Church and its institutions.

"Wherever the bishop shall appear, there let the multitude also be; even as, wherever Jesus Christ is, there is the Catholic Church."
—St. Ignatius of Antioch

Father John said, "I am like a man sitting under a great tree, who sees wild beasts and snakes coming against him in great numbers. When he cannot withstand them any longer, he runs to climb the tree and is saved. It is just the same with me. I sit in my prayer chamber and I am aware of evil thoughts coming against me. When I have no more strength against them, I take refuge in God by prayer and I am saved from the enemy."
—*The Wisdom of the Desert Fathers and Mothers*

October

"Let me realize that this time is being lent to me and it is not my own. I can rightly be called to account for this time if I am not prepared to devote it entirely to God."

—St. Teresa of Avila

What is your life dedicated toward? What are your goals? What do you want from your life? If God didn't appear in your answers to those questions, rededicate yourself to him right now.

"It is Jesus that you seek when you dream of happiness; He is waiting for you when nothing else you find satisfies you; He is the beauty to which you are so attracted; it is He who provoked you with that thirst for fullness that will not let you settle for compromise; it is He who urges you to shed the masks of a false life; it is He who reads in your hearts your most genuine choices, the choices that others try to stifle."

—Pope St. John Paul II

Jesus, I want to be happy. I want everyone I love to be happy. And I know that our happiness has its source in serving you.

"When you look at the crucifix, you understand how much Jesus loved you then. When you look at the Sacred Host, you understand how much Jesus loves you now."
—St. Teresa of Calcutta

Jesus, your love for me is overwhelming.
I will respond to your love by loving you
with my heart, mind, and actions, today.

Today is the feast day of Pope St. John Paul II.

"There is no place for selfishness and no place for fear! Do not be afraid, then, when love makes demands. Do not be afraid when love requires sacrifice."
—Pope St. John Paul II

"There is no evil to be faced that Christ does not face with us. There is no enemy that Christ has not already conquered. There is no cross to bear that Christ has not already born for us, and does not now bear with us."
—Pope St. John Paul II

Christ, defend me. Christ, lead me. Christ,
I am with you today and for the rest of my life!

"Consider it a sheer gift, friends, when tests and challenges come at you from all sides. You know that under pressure, your faith-life is forced into the open and shows its true colors. So don't try to get out of anything prematurely."

—JAMES 1:2–3 (MSG)

Are you testing me somehow, Jesus?

Meditating on the Cross of Christ, St. Teresa of Avila prayed: "Lord, if you are willing to suffer all this for me, what am I suffering for you? What do I have to complain about? I am ashamed, Lord, when I see you in such a situation. If there is any way I can imitate you I will suffer all trials that come to my way and count them as a great blessing. Lord, let us go together; wherever you go, I must go, and I must pass through whatever you pass."

What do you need to do today to serve God?

"I was right on the cliff-edge, ready to fall, when GOD grabbed and held me. God's my strength, he's also my song, and now he's my salvation."

—PSALM 118:12–14 (MSG)

I'm climbing up to you, God. Please hold my hand.

"The prophet said: I will stand on my watch and set my step on my tower, and I will watch to see what will be said to me. It is as if he were to say: I will stand on guard over my faculties and will take no step forward as to my actions, and so I will be able to contemplate what will be said to me—that is, I will understand and enjoy what is communicated to me supernaturally."

—St. John of the Cross

Ask God to speak in the quiet of your soul.

"You say you are anxious about the future, but don't you know that the Lord is with you always and that our enemy has no power over one who has resolved to belong entirely to Jesus?"

St. Pio of Pietrelcina

Don't worry about anything. The Lord is with you. Give yourself entirely to Jesus, today.

"Read some chapter of a devout book. . . . It is very easy and most necessary, for just as you speak to God when at prayer, God speaks to you when you read."

—St. Vincent de Paul

October

What are you currently reading—not at school, but at home? Remember what Pope Francis said: Read the Gospels for two minutes a day. Consider also how you spend your other time reading. It is fine to read for fun. But read some of the spiritual classics, too. You are never too young to discover books like St. Augustine's *Confessions*, or Brother Lawrence's *The Practice of the Presence of God*.

"Do good everywhere, so that everyone can say, 'this is a son of Christ.'"

—St. Pio of Pietrelcina

Christ Jesus, show me where to spread your love today.
I want to represent you to people that I meet, today.

"All of a creation is a song of praise to God."
—St. Hildegard of Bingen

Listen to the word around you—natural sounds of Creation—throughout the day today. Pay attention to what you often take for granted.

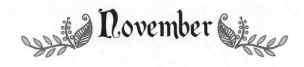

November

Today is the Feast of All Saints

"Remembering the prayer of Elisha to his father Elijah when he dared to ask for a double portion of his spirit [2 Kings 2:9], I presented myself before the Angels and the Saints, and I told them, 'I am the littlest of creatures, I know my wretchedness and my weakness, but I also know how much noble and generous hearts love to do good. I beg you, then, you Blessed inhabitants of heaven, I beg you to adopt me as your child. . . . It is foolhardy, I know, but nonetheless I dare to ask you to obtain this for me: a double portion of your Love.'"

—St. Thérèse of Lisieux

"You may say that if you had seen our Lord with your bodily eyes when he was living in the world, you would have gazed at him forever. Do not believe it. Anyone who will not make the effort to gaze upon this Lord present within her, which she can do with little trouble or danger, would not be likely to have stood at the foot of the cross with Saint Mary Magdalene, who looked death straight in the face."

—St. Teresa of Avila

Give me courage, today, Lord, to stand beside you—
even if that makes me feel uncomfortable.

November

"How sweet is the path of love. No doubt, one can fall down, one can commit unfaithful acts, but love, knowing how to profit from everything, quickly consumes everything that can be displeasing to Jesus, leaving only a humble and profound peace in the depths of the heart."
—St. Thérèse of Lisieux

I make mistakes, Lord. But I love you.

Today is the feast day of St. Charles Borromeo.

"If a tiny spark of God's love already burns within you, do not expose it to the wind, for it may get blown out. Keep the stove tightly shut so that it will not lose its heat and grow cold. In other words, avoid distractions as well as you can."
—St. Charles Borromeo

Guard your spark carefully. Don't expose it to the wind, where it might get blown out. What is the "wind" in your life?

Your word is a lamp to my feet and a light to my path.
—Psalm 119:105 (ESV)

Holy Spirit, open Your holy Gospel to me. Help me understand.

Do not be deceived; God is not mocked,
for you reap whatever you sow.
—GALATIANS 6:7 (NRSV)

What are you trying to hide from God? Do you think it works—
to hide it from him?

[Jesus said,] "Here's what I want you to do: Find a quiet, secluded
place so you won't be tempted to role-play before God. Just be
there as simply and honestly as you can manage. The focus will
shift from you to God, and you will begin to sense his grace."
—MATTHEW 6:6 (MSG)

"It might also help to have a good book, written in simple
language, to help you in your prayer habits. With such an aid
you will learn your vocal prayers well, and little by little your soul
will get used to this. . . . Stay at [the] good Master's side, and be
determined to learn what he teaches you."
—ST. TERESA OF AVILA

Listen to a saint: "It is always a great thing to base your prayer on
prayers that the Lord spoke with his own lips."
—ST. TERESA OF AVILA

This is why we pray: *Our Father, who art in Heaven. . . .*

November

"I was to pass through many trials, but the Divine call was so pressing that even if I had had to pass through flames, I would have done so in order to be faithful to Jesus."

—St. Thérèse of Lisieux

We rarely go through the kind of trials that saints and martyrs went through. We rarely suffer for our faith the way they did. But we need to be prepared for if that time ever comes. Will you be ready to stay faithful to Christ even if your faith is challenged?

Let me give you a new command: Love one another. In the same way I loved you, you love one another. This is how everyone will recognize that you are my disciples—when they see the love you have for each other.

—John 13:34–35 (MSG)

As the members of a team all wear the same jersey or uniform, those who are truly Christians love each other. And that is how we know we are Christians: by our love.

"Do not be afraid. Do not be satisfied with mediocrity. Put out into the deep and let down your nets for a catch."
—POPE ST. JOHN PAUL II

Are you willing to take risks for God? What would that mean in your life? How can you serve him today in a way that is "risky"?

On this day in 354, St. Augustine was born in northern Africa, then part of the Roman Empire. He would write these famous words in his autobiography (one of the first autobiographies ever written), "Our hearts were made for You, O Lord, and they are restless until they rest in you."
—ST. AUGUSTINE OF HIPPO

My heart is restless today, Lord. Help me see you more clearly.

Today is the feast day of St. Frances Xavier Cabrini. She is sometimes also called "Mother Cabrini." She was the first U.S. citizen to be canonized.

"We must pray without tiring, for the salvation of mankind does not depend upon material success, nor on sciences that cloud the intellect. Neither does it depend on arms and human industries, but on Jesus alone."
—ST. FRANCES CABRINI

"Give something, however small, to the one in need. For it is not small to one who has nothing. Neither is it small to God, if we have given what we could."

—St. Gregory Nazianzen

God, show me how to give today. Show me to whom I should give, today.

"What really matters in life is that we are loved by Christ and that we love him in return. In comparison to the love of Jesus, everything else is secondary. And, without the love of Jesus, everything is useless."

—Pope St. John Paul II

Jesus, I love you. No other love matters as much to me as yours does.

"Prayer is the oxygen of the soul."

—St. Pio of Pietrelcina

You are learning science in school, right? Have you learned about oxygen? What can't you do without oxygen? What, then, would the saint mean by saying that prayer is the "oxygen" of the soul?

The Lord gives strength to his people;
the Lord blesses his people with peace.
—Psalm 29:11 (NIV)

I know that You want me to simply be myself with You.

"Genuine love . . . is demanding. But its beauty lies precisely in the demands it makes. Only those able to make demands on themselves in the name of love can then demand love from others."
—Pope St. John Paul II

We want to be loved by others. Perhaps you easily feel the love of parents, siblings, friends. But not everyone does. Be thankful for the love in your life today.

"Stay quiet with God. Do not spend your time in useless chatter."
—St. Charles Borromeo

This is tough for kids—kids are supposed to play, and what an adult might call "chatter" is what a kid might call "play." But consider, today, how can you, in some special ways, stay quiet with God?

November

Saints often offer prayers to God that praise and thank God using different names than those we normally use in Church. St. Hildegard of Bingen, for instance, once prayed: "Holy Wisdom, Soaring Power, encompass us with wings unfurled, and carry us, encircling all, above, below, and through the world."

Offer your own prayer to God right now. It is okay to use new words. . . .

21

Don't be fooled by people who say that the devil is not real. Our Church teaches, and the Bible makes it clear, that the devil is active around us, trying to get us to do wrong.

But, listen to a saint: "Remember this forever: it is a healthy sign if the devil shouts and roars around your conscience, since this shows that he is not inside your will."
> —ST. PIO OF PIETRELCINA

22

"Prayer is the best weapon we have; it is the key to God's heart. You must speak to Jesus not only with your lips, but with your heart. In fact, on certain occasions you should only speak to Him with your heart."
> —ST. PIO OF PIETRELCINA

I will pray to you throughout the day today, Lord, with my heart.

There are very good reasons why we pray, why we go to Mass, why we obey God in big and small things.

"The field of battle between God and Satan is the human soul. It is in the soul that the battle rages every moment of life."
—St. Pio of Pietrelcina

The Spirit helps us in our weakness. We do not know what we ought to pray for, but the Spirit himself intercedes for us through wordless groans.
—Romans 8:26 (NIV)

God, what can I say? Help me, please!?

Do not love the world or anything in the world. If anyone loves the world, love for the Father is not in them.
—1 John 2:15 (NIV)

"There are many nowadays whose reason is darkened to spiritual things by greed. They serve money and not God and are influenced by money and not by God. They put the cost of a thing first, and not its divine worth and reward."
—St. John of the Cross

Holy Spirit, if I am loving the wrong things, show me.

November

26

I am God, the only God there is. Besides me there are no real gods. I'm the one who armed you for this work.

—Isaiah 45:5 (msg)

"What sweet joy it is to think that God is just—that is, that he takes into account our weakness and knows perfectly the fragility of our nature. What should I be afraid of?"

—St. Thérèse of Lisieux

27

My child, if you accept my words . . . making your ear attentive to wisdom and inclining your heart to understanding . . . then you will understand the fear of the Lord and find the knowledge of God.

—Proverbs 2:1, 2, 5 (nrsv)

I will guard my ears today, Lord.

28

Long before he laid down earth's foundations, he had us in mind, had settled on us as the focus of his love, to be made whole and holy by his love. Long, long ago he decided to adopt us into his family through Jesus Christ.

—EPHESIANS 1:4–5 (MSG)

Dear God, you know me better than I know myself.
Show me the way today!

29

"The biggest disease is not leprosy or tuberculosis, but rather the feeling of being unwanted."

—ST. TERESA OF CALCUTTA

Reach out today, and be a friend, to someone at school or in your neighborhood who feels unwanted.

30

"Let us always meet each other with a smile, for the smile is the beginning of love."

—ST. TERESA OF CALCUTTA

Practice smiling more often today. It's easy!

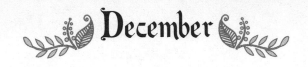

December

1

"Rejoice and be glad that so great a Lord came into a Virgin's womb, willing to be poor and despised in this world, so that we who are poor and despised can become rich in him."
—St. Clare of Assisi

Most of us aren't poor, at least not in the way that many people in the world are poor today. Jesus and the first disciples were intentionally poor. Jesus asked those who wanted to follow him to give up everything—including their stuff, their security. Would you be prepared to do that, too, for Christ?

2

Live by the Spirit.
—Galatians 5:16 (nrsv)

God said to St. Catherine of Siena: "I have told you that a holy desire is a continual prayer." What is your continual prayer today?

"No one heals himself by wounding another."
—St. Ambrose of Milan

Remember this throughout your day. This is not only the teaching of saints, but the wisdom of good teachers and parents everywhere. Who could you compliment, rather than criticize, today?

"The Blessed Virgin made me feel that it was truly she who had smiled at me and had healed me. I understood that she was watching over me, that I was her child, so that I could no longer call her anything but Mama, because that name seemed even more tender than that of Mother."
—St. Thérèse of Lisieux

Hail Mary. . . .

December

Many theologians will say that the most profound spiritual writing of all, of any of the saints anywhere, anytime, is what we know as the Magnificat—also known as the Song of Mary, recorded in the Gospel of Luke, chapter 1. Pray these words today with the Virgin Mother:

My soul proclaims the greatness of the Lord,
my spirit rejoices in God my Savior,
for he has looked with favor on his humble servant.
From this day all generations will call me blessed,
the Almighty has done great things for me,
and holy is his Name.
He has mercy on those who fear Him
in every generation.
He has shown the strength of his arm,
he has scattered the proud in their conceit.
He has cast down the mighty from their thrones,
and has lifted up the humble.
He has filled the hungry with good things,
and the rich he has sent away empty.
He has come to the help of his servant Israel
for he has remembered his promise of mercy,
the promise he made to our fathers,
to Abraham and his children for ever.
Glory to the Father, and to the Son, and to the Holy Spirit,
as it was in the beginning, is now, and will be for ever.

Today is the feast day of St. Nicholas of Myra, a fourth-century bishop who is the real-life model for what became Santa Claus ("St. Nick"). St. Nicholas was always looking for ways to help people in need.

One time, he heard of a man with three daughters, and how poor they were. Nicholas decided to help, but being too humble to help them publicly, he went to the house at night and threw three purses, each filled with gold coins, down the chimney.

"God, the giver of every good and perfect gift has called upon us to mimic that giving, by grace, through faith. This is not of ourselves."

—St. Nicholas of Myra

I can't give your love, God, without your grace and your help.
Help me, today.

December

8

"Consider that although we may consider ourselves righteous and frequently succeed in deceiving others, we can conceal nothing from God. So, we should strive to preserve the holiness of our souls and to guard the purity of our bodies with all fervor."
—St. Nicholas of Myra

What does holiness mean to you? Are there any ways in which you are trying to deceive God and yourself by being other than holy?

9

"We become what we love and who we love shapes what we become."
—St. Clare of Assisi

Take a few minutes today to make a list of what you love. This saint says, "We become what we love." Then, look at your list again. Does your list of loves express what you want to become?

10

Brother Lawrence, who was a lay brother in a monastery in Paris 350 years ago, once said, "You don't need to cry very loud. God is always nearer to us than we think."

God, I know you are right here with me. You hear me.
I'm glad that you are my Friend, my Savior, my Comforter.

"Be a Catholic: When you kneel before an altar, do it in such a way that others may be able to recognize that you know before whom you kneel."
—St. Maximilian Kolbe

What do you think the saint meant by this? How would the way you use your body in prayer, or at Mass, show people that you know before whom you are kneeling?

We are fools for the sake of Christ, but you are wise in Christ. We are weak, but you are strong.
—1 Corinthians 4:10 (NRSV)

Our parents encourage us to be smart and strong, don't they? They want us to succeed, to do well. But we have to remember, still, that it is okay—it is even good—to be foolish and weak before God. We *are* weak compared to God, and we always will be.

December

You correct little by little those who trespass, and you remind and warn them of the things through which they sin, so that they may . . . put their trust in you.
—WISDOM 12:1–2 (NRSV)

"You will probably laugh at me and say how obvious such things are. But, until I closed my eyes to the vanities of this world, I did not see or understand who lived within my soul or what my soul deserved. If I had understood then, as I now do, how this great King lives within this palace of my soul, I would not have left him alone so much."
—ST. TERESA OF AVILA

Jesus was born in stable, not a palace, born of a humble woman, not a queen. Listen to the saint: "By bringing Himself low in this way, God shows His infinite greatness. Just as the sun shines at the same time on the tall cedars and on each little flower as if it were the only one on earth, in the same way Our Lord is concerned particularly for every soul as if there were none other like it."
—ST. THÉRÈSE OF LISIEUX

God, I love how you love me!

St. Antony the Great taught: "Let Christians care for nothing that they cannot take away with them. We ought rather to seek after that which will lead us to heaven, namely wisdom, chastity, justice, virtue, an ever-watchful mind, care of the poor, firm faith in Christ, a mind that can control anger, and hospitality. Striving after these things, we shall prepare for ourselves a dwelling in the land of the peaceful, as it says in the Gospel."

I am focusing on virtue, today, on doing your work in the world, God.

Pray today with the words of St. Augustine of Hippo:

"All of the things in the world that are not God, are stuff I don't want. Holy Spirit, powerful Consoler, sacred bond of the Father and the Son, come into my heart and establish in it your loving home. Kindle in my lazy soul the fire of your love so that I may be completely on fire for you."

Look around you today, even if, after school, the skies are becoming dark much earlier than they were a few months ago. Look at the stars and pray this prayer with St. Francis of Assisi:

"Praised be you, my Lord, for sister Moon and the Stars: in the heavens you formed them, clear, precious and beautiful."

December

Sometimes our greatest prayer can be simply expressing awe and wonder at how beautiful the world is that God created. Thank God today for that beauty.

> "Most High, all powerful, good Lord,
> to you all praise, glory and honor and all blessing;
> to you alone, Most High, belongs all praise."
> —ST. FRANCIS OF ASSISI

Remember your guardian angel, put there by God to watch over you.

"Be good. This will make your angel happy. When sorrows and misfortunes, physical or spiritual, afflict you, turn to your guardian angel with real trust and he will help you."
—ST. JOHN BOSCO

Thank you, God, for watching over me.

20

"We desire to be able to welcome Jesus at Christmastime, not in a cold manger of our heart, but in a heart full of love and humility, in a heart so pure, so immaculate, so warm with love for one another."

—St. Teresa of Calcutta

On this Holy Night, prepare your heart to be a place where Jesus Christ might find warmth. Just as Jesus was born in a stable long ago, he wants to be born in each of our hearts, today.

21

St. Joseph, the husband of Mary, is an often-ignored saint at Christmastime. Go read the text in the Gospels about Joseph's relationship to Mary's son. He was essentially a foster father—a relationship that many of us can relate to, today. Yet, he loved this son as his very own.

St. Joseph, pray for me.

December

St. Joseph was chosen to be the protector of Mary, her husband, her lifelong companion and partner. He is the patron saint of fathers. You can pray to St. Joseph. Ask him to pray from heaven for your father, today.

"Saint Joseph was a just man, a tireless worker, the upright guardian of those entrusted to his care. May he always guard, protect and enlighten families."
—POPE JOHN PAUL II

Christmas is coming very soon now. We anticipate. We wait. Just be sure that you are anticipating and waiting for what is most important: the coming of Christ.

"Jesus was my first love," St. Teresa of Calcutta used to say. You've heard all about what incredible things she did, dedicating her life to serving the poor in India. We can't all be Mother Teresas, but we can allow Jesus's love, and our love for Jesus, to transform our lives until we, too, do something incredible for God.

December

Consider St. Joseph one more time, just now, on Christmas Eve. The angel came to Joseph and asked him to accept the mysterious pregnancy that had taken place in the woman to whom he was engaged. How difficult that must have been for Joseph to accept! Then, he had a dream, and in that dream, God explained it to him.

Joseph never could have accepted God's mystery and grace if Joseph had not first of all listened carefully. It is difficult to listen, today, with so much going on around us, and in our ears. Listen tonight. Listen for God. . . .

Christmas Day today! Sometimes the best way to pray is by singing. Sing a Christmas hymn as your prayer, today. And listen to a saint: "Today the darkness begins to grow shorter and the light to lengthen, as the hours of night become fewer. Realize that the true light is now here and, through the rays of the gospel, is illumining the whole earth."

—St. Gregory of Nyssa

December

"In the end, everything else will turn out to be unimportant and unessential, except for this: Father, Child, and Love."
—St. Pope John Paul II

In the excitement of Christmas, and presents and food and family, be sure to remember what is important. Today is the Feast of St. Stephen, the first martyr of Christianity, sometimes called St. Stephen's Day. Perhaps you've sung the Christmas carol "Good King Wenceslaus," which tells of Wenceslaus going out on the Feast of Stephen to do charity. Today is a day when all of us should do something for those less fortunate.

Pope Francis recently said on Christmas Day: "The power of this Child, Son of God and Son of Mary, is not the power of this world, based on might and wealth; it is the power of love." This is one of the most important ways of understanding what Christmas is all about: love.

Jesus, I will love you in the new year more than I ever have, before.

Try making a list of what you will do in the new year to love people around you.

28

"It is Christmas every time you let God love others through you."
—St. Teresa of Calcutta

At Christmastime, and all the time, this is the most common theme from the lives and teachings of the saints: love. Our entire lives as Christians can be summarized as being about this one thing: love.

29

Today is the feast day of St. Thomas Becket, a martyr who was murdered by a king in medieval England. Listen to the saint:

"Remember the sufferings of Christ, the storms that were weathered . . . the crown that came from those sufferings which gave new radiance to the faith. All saints give testimony to the truth that without real effort, no one ever wins the crown."
—St. Thomas Becket

30

To love means to do real things in the world. It isn't just a feeling. Listen to the saint:

"Above all, remember that God looks for solid virtues in us, such as patience, humility, obedience, abnegation of your own will—that is, the good will to serve him and our neighbor in him."
—St. Ignatius of Loyola

31

[Jesus said,] "For the gate is narrow and the road is hard that leads to life, and there are few who find it."
—Matthew 7:14 (NRSV)

"Our Savior says first that the gate is narrow, to make it clear that in order for the soul to enter by this gate, which is Christ, and which comes at the beginning of the road, the will must first be narrowed ... and it must love God above them all."
—St. John of the Cross

I am narrowing my will, Lord.
I am focusing more than ever on following you,
and loving you, closely. Amen.

Closing Prayer

"The saints now in God's presence preserve their bonds of love and communion with us. The Book of Revelation attests to this when it speaks of the intercession of the martyrs: 'I saw under the altar the souls of those who had been slain for the word of God and for the witness they had borne; they cried out with a loud voice, "O sovereign Lord, holy and true, how long will it be before you judge?"' (6:9–10). Each of us can say: 'Surrounded, led and guided by the friends of God . . . I do not have to carry alone what, in truth, I could never carry alone. All the saints of God are there to protect me, to sustain me and to carry me.'"

—POPE FRANCIS,
from his apostolic exhortation *Gaudete et Exsultate* (No. 4)

You may also be interested in . . .